Australian Army Campa

MW01485843

AUSTRALIAN MILITARY OPERATIONS IN VIETNAM

Second Edition

ALBERT PALAZZO

ARMY·HISTORY·UNIT

PROTECTING ARMY HERITAGE
PROMOTING ARMY HISTORY

2011

©Copyright Army History Unit
Campbell Park Offices (CP2-5-166)
Canberra ACT 2600
AUSTRALIA
(02) 6266 4248
(02) 6266 4044 – fax

First published 2006 – Second Edition 2009
Reprinted 2011

National Library of Australia Cataloguing-in-Publication entry

Author: Palazzo, Albert, 1957-
Title: Australian military operations in Vietnam
Edition: 2nd ed.
ISBN: 9780980475388 (pbk.)
Series: Australian army campaigns series; 3
Notes: Includes index. Bibliography.
Subjects: Vietnam War, 1961-1975 – Participation, Australian.
            Vietnam War, 1961-1975 – Campaigns.

Dewey Number: 959.7043394

Typesetting by Margaret McNally, Canberra, ACT
Printed and bound in Malaysia for Imago

Front Cover: AWM EKN/70/0468/VN
Back Cover: AWM FOD/71/0255/VN; THU/68/0273/VN; FAI/70/0169/VN; FOD/71/0305/VN
Title Page: AWM CUN/66/0475/VN

CONTENTS

ACKNOWLEDGEMENTS

In the course of researching and writing *Australian Military Operations in Vietnam* I incurred debts to a number of institutions and individuals. This work was an initiative of the Army History Unit and its members have my thanks for its place in the Australian Army Campaigns Series. At the Australian War Memorial I must thank the staff of the research centre, in particular David Jolliffe who played a key role in locating vital records. Mr Roger Rees at the Defence Imagery and Geospatial Organisation has my thanks for his provision of topographical maps. I must also thank Captain John Landis of the Royal Australian Infantry Corps Museum for permission to photograph the collection's Vietnam era weapons.

A number of specialists have contributed to this book. Mark Wahlert was responsible for the book's illustrations and 3-D maps, Kay Dancey and Anthony Bright prepared the 2-D maps, and Jeff Isaacs, OAM, painted the artwork. Research assistance was provided by Jean Bou and Michael Molkentin. Mike also prepared the index. Ian Kuring provided insight into weaponry and shared his experience with MATT. Glenn Wahlert contributed the weapon data inserts. The cover design was the work of Catherine McCulloch of Defence Publishing Service.

My wife, Melissa Benyon, once again read and commented on the book's draft. My son, Thomas Palazzo, analysed the companion computer game and provided youthful insights into its playability. Cathy McCullagh undertook the book's copyedit, and Margaret McNally did the typeset.

The book's development was materially eased by the efforts of Glenn Wahlert, the project manager of the Australian Army Campaigns Series. Again, Glenn has my thanks.

Albert Palazzo
Consultant Historian, Canberra
August 2006

ACKNOWLEDGEMENTS – SECOND EDITION

The author would like to thank Roger Lee of the Army History Unit for the opportunity to write a second edition of this book. Several people have played a key role in its revision. In particular the author would like to acknowledge the assistance of Ian Kuring, Mark Wahlert, Margaret McNally, Albert M. Palazzo and Melissa Benyon.

Albert Palazzo
Senior Research Fellow
Land Warfare Studies Centre
November 2008

AUSTRALIAN MILITARY OPERATIONS IN VIETNAM

THE ORIGINS OF THE VIETNAM CONFLICT

Australia and South-East Asia.
Anthony Bright.

Background to the Vietnam War

The origins of Australia's involvement in the Vietnam War lay in the collapse of French authority over the region during and after the Second World War. European contact with Vietnam dated from the 16th century with the arrival of merchants and missionaries. It was not until 1858 that France began a military conquest of Vietnam and the adjoining kingdoms of Cambodia and Laos, a process which it did not complete until 1893. The French divided their possessions into five colonies and protectorates: Cochinchina, Annam, and Tonkin (together making up Vietnam), Cambodia and Laos. French control of Vietnam was, therefore, a relatively recent event, and came about only through the displacement of long-standing indigenous sovereignty.

In their short time as the colonial masters of South-East Asia the French did not develop an enviable reputation. Naturally, they ruled for the benefit of Paris, directing Vietnam's wealth to France while using the region as a market for the home country's manufactured goods. Colonial administrators forced villagers off their land in order to provide labour for plantations and mines, and kept the peasants in poverty through high taxes, exorbitant rents, and exploitation by rice brokers. The French also sought to break down Vietnamese local identity by imposing European language, culture and religion.

Opposition to the French was feeble, and the Europeans quickly and brutally suppressed the few rebellions that did erupt. The colonial government also suppressed indigenous-based political parties and forced them underground. One of these parties was the Indochina Communist Party that Ho Chi Minh founded in 1930. Ho was a charismatic leader, and the party's call for national independence and social equality were well-aimed policy goals. The Indochina Communist Party remained an insignificant force throughout the 1930s, its members numbering only in the hundreds and scattered across South-East Asia. However, it would be the communists who would become the eventual rulers of Vietnam, emerging victorious from lengthy wars against first France and then the United States.

The Indochina Communist Party took advantage of the power vacuum created in Indochina by the Second World War to advance its cause. In 1940, after a brief campaign, France fell to Nazi Germany leaving its Indochinese territories vulnerable to a militarist and expansionist Japan. The Japanese were quick to act on French weakness. At first Japan demanded only concessions such as port access from Indochina's colonial administrators, but gradually its forces occupied all of South-East Asia. For most of the Pacific War the French technically continued to administer Indochina, but their control was a thin veneer behind which lay Japanese military might. This arrangement suited the Japanese, who did not fully remove the French until almost the end of the war. However it tainted the colonial administrators as collaborators.

In May 1941 Ho founded the Viet Minh (Front for the Independence of Vietnam) which became one of the leading opposition groups to the Japanese and their French lackeys. Espousing Vietnamese nationalism, the Viet Minh sought the withdrawal of both foreign overlords and the establishment of an independent nation. At its peak, and with some aid—albeit slight—from the American Office of Strategic Services, the Viet Minh controlled only a small part of Vietnam. Its authority extended only as far as the mountainous provinces of Tonkin near the border with China. Ho avoided military confrontation because he did not want to risk annihilation, a fate which befell other Vietnamese resistance groups. Instead, the recruitment of cadres and the building of an organisation were his priorities.

The French Indochina War

With Japan's defeat Ho moved to take charge of Vietnam. Across Tonkin, Viet Minh agents assumed control of towns and villages, and in Hanoi, Indochina Communist Party operators occupied the government buildings vacated by the Japanese. On 2 September 1945 Ho delivered an address in Hanoi in which he declared the establishment of the Democratic Republic of Vietnam and asked the free world to recognise the country's freedom and independence. Ho did not have a mandate from the Vietnamese people for his actions, but he had moved quickly, seizing the initiative and the organs of government.

France, however, was unwilling to acquiesce to the loss of Indochina. In October 1945 a French expeditionary force arrived to re-establish colonial authority. As the Viet Minh did not have a strong presence in the south, the French easily occupied Saigon and resumed control of Cochinchina and much of Annam. Tonkin, however, was a different matter. On 28 November fighting broke out between French and Viet Minh troops in Haiphong, Hanoi's port, initiating a conflict that did not cease until 1954.

While France wanted the jewel of its colonial empire back, it did not have the will to wage a major war. Despite the home country's provision of insufficient troops and inadequate support, French commanders in Vietnam did achieve some success against the Viet Minh. Whenever seriously threatened, however, the communists withdrew to their mountain strongholds, only to emerge again later to strike at French weakness. The Viet Minh, under the guidance of their brilliant general Giap Vo Nguyen, slowly sapped French will and strength, while also building a professional, well-armed and -led force that was able to conduct both insurgency and conventional warfare operations with equal effectiveness.

The United States did provide some military assistance to France, but its support was always conditional. The United States was caught in a quandary. While France was a traditional ally, and despite the United States needing French help in the rebuilding and rearming of Europe against the Soviet Union, America remained strongly opposed to the re-establishment of colonialism. Consequently, American aid was never as great, or as freely given, as it might have been.

In mid-1953, France and the Viet Minh drifted towards negotiations. The new French commander, General Henri Navarre, hoped that a military victory would influence the talks in France's favour. He chose as his battleground the isolated valley of Dien Bien Phu, near the Laotian border with Tonkin and in the heart of the enemy territory. Navarre's plan was twofold. First, the French occupation of Dien Bien Phu would interdict communist communications with Laos, thereby easing the pressure on that colony's hard-pressed garrison. Second, it would lure the Viet Minh into a decisive battle in which the French would destroy the enemy force with firepower.

Navarre seriously miscalculated the capabilities of both his forces and those of his enemy. On 20 November 1953, French paratroopers descended into the valley of Dien Bien Phu and began construction of a fire base. Their only link to Hanoi and French-controlled territory was via the air.

Giap did not attack immediately. Instead he painstakingly built up a defensive ring around the garrison and dug in guns on the ridges overlooking the French. On 12 March the battle began, and the defenders soon learned that they were outnumbered, outgunned and outclassed. They also learned the limitations of a distantly deployed force dependent on an air bridge for its maintenance. Once the Viet Minh gunners came within range of the airstrip the battle was lost, although the garrison's agony continued until its capitulation on 7 May when 12,000 French troops laid down their arms. The following day France began negotiations in earnest with the Viet Minh in Geneva.

> **Lesson 1**
>
> Logistics determine what is possible in war. To send troops into a distant theatre without properly considering the practicalities of their support is to ensure defeat. While air bridges permit long-ranged insertions they are especially vulnerable to interdiction, either by enemy action or the elements.
> Once a deployed force loses its link to its support base it faces defeat if not destruction.

The United States and the Slide towards War

The Geneva Agreement of July 1954 divided Vietnam into two countries: a communist north and a free south, separated along the 17th Parallel. The agreement also called for a free national election to determine the political future of the Vietnamese people.

The Viet Minh would almost certainly have won an election had one been held. Their victory over the French had given the communists great prestige among their people. Moreover, they already had a well-developed organisation in place, unlike the nascent South Vietnamese government of Ngo Dinh Diem. Furthermore, Diem's rule had more than a whiff of illegitimacy about it. As the war's end neared, the French puppet emperor, Bao Dai, had appointed Diem Prime Minister. Diem lacked a support base and his rule became increasingly corrupt, inefficient and brutal. In 1954, however, he was the United States' best option, and earned that country's support by default.

The United States did not want to chance a risky election and moved to undermine the terms of the Geneva Agreement. The day after its announcement, the American Secretary of State, John Foster Dulles, pronounced, 'the remaining free areas of Indochina must be built up if the dike against Communism is to be held.' In accordance with the accepted 'domino theory', the United States feared that if South Vietnam fell to communism the rest of South-East Asia would soon follow. Therefore, the United States embarked on a policy of financial and military advisory assistance to the Diem regime.

To further shore up support for South Vietnam, the United States established the South-East Asia Treaty Organisation (SEATO). SEATO was a regional defence agreement to which Australia was a signatory. The French remained in South Vietnam until the second half of 1955, but growing American involvement curtailed their influence.

President Ngo Dinh Diem greets Air Marshal V. E. Hancock in Saigon in 1963. Between them is the Australian Ambassador to South Vietnam, B. C. Hill.
AWM P01943.001.

The Start of the American War

During the 1960s the political situation in South Vietnam deteriorated rapidly. In part, this was a result of the power struggle within Vietnam; but it was also due to the incompetency and repressiveness of the Diem government. Assassins removed Diem in November 1963, and a series of coups followed, resulting in 'revolving door' government. Stability did not return until General Thieu Nguyen Van seized power in June 1965.

Well before his murder, Diem had managed to alienate nearly every sector of South Vietnamese society. In 1959, sensing the South's frailty, the North Vietnamese Central Committee authorised the commencement of 'protracted armed struggle' to overthrow the Diem–United States regime. In that year, Hanoi began the construction of the Ho Chi Minh trail, and communist soldiers headed south to assist the growing network of cadres and insurgents in South Vietnam. By 1961, guerrilla warfare was widespread across South Vietnam.

Taking advantage of the instability following Diem's assassination, the communists escalated the infiltration of the South, including the deployment of field units. Against better led and motivated Viet Cong[†] (VC) units the Army of the Republic of Vietnam (ARVN) performed poorly. The situation deteriorated to the point that any movement outside Saigon required a large escort to ensure the safety of those involved.

The United States attempted to counteract the worsening situation in South Vietnam by increasing its assistance. By 1963 there were 16,000 American military advisers in the country. Even with this aid, however, the South Vietnamese could not stem the North's onslaught. VC field units of regimental size appeared, and the communists unleashed coordinated offensives. When the ARVN took on the VC, the South Vietnamese invariably suffered heavy losses. Towards the end of 1964, for example, the VC infiltrated the village of Binh Gia in Phuoc Tuy Province. The ARVN relief force lost 201 soldiers killed in action (KIA) in forcing them out.

---

† NOTE: The Communists fielded a wide array of different types of units in the war against the South. These consisted of locally raised guerrilla groups at the village, district and provincial level, main force field units, and, lastly, regular units of the People's Army of Vietnam. The capabilities of these units varied widely, ranging from lightly equipped insurgents to heavily armed conventional forces. The make-up of these forces also varied, and it was not uncommon for a unit raised in the South to contain a high percentage of personnel who had infiltrated from the North. In fact, over time this percentage increased. What must be noted, however, is that despite their origins, organisation, capability, purpose or identifying name, the various types of Communist forces operating in the South followed the central direction of Communist government in Hanoi in the North. In order to simplify the identification of such a wide array of opposition, this book will employ the generic term 'Viet Cong' to describe the enemies which the Australian soldier fought.

By early 1965 the United States faced a stark choice: intervene militarily or concede the loss of South Vietnam to communism. Without direct American military assistance, the fall of Saigon was only a few months off.

In February 1965, United States aircraft began to bomb targets in North Vietnam, and the following month United States Marine and Army combat units deployed to the South. The American President, Lyndon B. Johnson, had decided to fight for Vietnam. The United States was at war.

Australia's Decision to Enter the War

Shortly after Johnson dispatched ground forces to Vietnam the Australian Prime Minister, Robert Menzies, reached a similar decision. On 29 April 1965 he announced to Parliament that Australia would join the war. Members of the Australian Army Training Team Vietnam (AATTV) had been in South Vietnam since 1962 serving as advisers, but now Australia was to commit combat troops.

Menzies' motivation behind his decision to intervene was not complex. He accepted that Australia sat isolated in a part of the globe where security threats were particularly evident. Australia was already involved in an undeclared war with Indonesia on the island of Borneo, and the threat of escalation into open conflict was palpable. Menzies shared the United States' opposition to communism and a belief in the need to contain its spread. The Australian Prime Minister also subscribed to the domino theory and feared that all of South-East Asia would cascade into communism if South Vietnam gave way. He was also concerned that the loss of South Vietnam would increase pressure on Malaya, where Australian forces had only recently helped defeat another communist insurgency.

Menzies accepted that the cornerstone of Australian defence policy was the maintenance of a close security relationship with the United States. Relationships are two-sided, however, and if Australia were to receive American military assistance when required, it had to be seen as willing to help the United States in return. It was Australia's participation in the Korean War, for example, that encouraged the United States to agree to the ANZUS Treaty. Thus an element of Australia's readiness to join the United States in Vietnam must be viewed from the perspective of what has been referred to as the 'insurance policy'.

STRATEGIES IN CONFLICT

The Vietnamese Communist and Revolutionary Struggle

The Viet Minh were veterans of insurgency warfare, having used it first to vanquish France and then to undermine the nascent government of South Vietnam. They would also use its principles to defeat the United States and its Australian ally.

According to communist theory, an insurgency campaign has three distinct phases: the passive phase, the active phase and the counter-offensive phase.

During the passive phase the insurgency's emphasis is on planning and the establishment of an organisation, primarily at the village level. While para-military units are formed, they limit their actions to propaganda, intimidation, assassination, sabotage and small-scale attacks on isolated government posts.

The commencement of the active phase sees an intensification in insurgency actions. The insurgents construct base areas, organise larger guerrilla units, increase attacks on government installations and create an administration structure that parallels that of the government.

During the counter-offensive phase the insurgency becomes overt and attempts to topple the now weakened government by force. Regular manoeuvre elements appear and undertake conventional warfare operations. The insurgency's leadership also encourages popular uprisings to bring down the government.

There is no prescribed timetable for the insurgency's advancement through these phases. Instead, success and opportunity serve as the guideposts. Moreover, failure, or stronger than expected opposition, simply results in the insurgents' reverting to lower levels of activity. Meanwhile, throughout each of these phases, the insurgents continue to build and nurture the movement's organisation.

One of the key differences between the objectives of an insurgency and those of conventional war is that the former's primary focus is on political operations that aim to win the support of the people, rather than destroy the enemy's military strength. The Chinese leader, Mao Tse-Tung, insisted that an insurgency had to organise and unite with the people because it was from the people that the movement garnered its support: recruits, food, labour, transportation, medical assistance and intelligence. For an insurgency, therefore, political values, not military operations, were the paramount concern.

Demilitarized Zone

LAOS

THAILAND

Ho Chi Minh Trail

CAMBODIA

Mekong River

Phnom Penh

SOUTH VIETNAM

I CORPS

II CORPS

III CORPS

IV CORPS

Quang Tri

Hue

Da Nang

Quang Ngai

Kontum

Cam Ranh

Saigon

Vung Tau

South China Sea

metres
2000
1500
1000
500
200
0

N

17°N

13°N

9°N

105°E   109°E

- - - - - International boundary

———— Corps TAOR boundary

0   100
kilometres

South Vietnam.
Anthony Bright.

13

Insurgents regard the conduct of battle and the control of territory as being of lesser value than does a conventional military force. Furthermore, insurgents do not believe that these two factors bring victory on their own. On this point Mao observed that, 'to gain territory is no cause for joy, and to lose territory is no cause for sorrow.' Moreover, Mao insisted that territory should be freely surrendered at an opponent's approach because by advancing, the enemy demonstrated its superior strength. According to communist doctrine, insurgents should only accept battle when they have a significant advantage. Otherwise, their doctrine requires them to break contact, disperse and re-form at an alternate position.

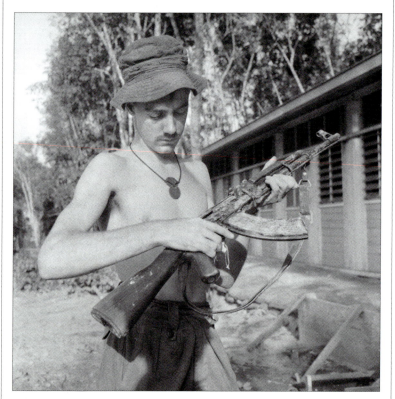

Private Murray Withers of 7 RAR examines an AK47.
AWM GIL/67/1191/VN.

Kalashnikov AK47, 7.62mm Assault Rifle (USSR) & Chicom Type 56 (PRC)

Calibre: 7.62 mm
Action:
 Magazine fed, gas operation, selective fire – semi automatic and automatic fire
Length: 870 mm
Weight: 4.3 kg empty
Muzzle velocity: 710 m/sec
Magazine capacity:
 30 round box/ 75 round drum
Cyclic rate of fire: 600 rpm
Effective range: 300 m

The AK47 (Avtomat Kalashnikova) is among the most successful weapons ever produced and remains in use by many armies, especially in the Third World. It is renowned for its ruggedness, durability, reliability, simplicity and ease of use. The AK47, along with the Chinese copy—the Chicom Type 56—was one of the favoured weapons of the VC throughout the Vietnam War.

A Russian manufactured AK47 (Avtomat Kalashnikova). RAICM

Since territory is of minor significance in an insurgency conflict, combatants cannot define the battlespace with traditional terms such as front lines, combat zones, lines of communication and rear areas. To do so would emphasise the importance of the land rather than the people. Instead, in Vietnam, units operated on isolated 360° battlefields against an opponent who could strike from any direction.

The critical individual in the communist insurgency concept of war is the cadre. The cadre is the movement's local leader and generally comes from the village in which he or she works. The cadre's tasks are numerous but include duties such as improving the local logistic and intelligence networks; working with youth groups to encourage them to join guerrilla units; instigating acts of sabotage; improving the care of wounded insurgents and assuring proper burial for the dead; increasing agricultural production from which the insurgency draws its food; and conducting indoctrination sessions. In a sense the cadre's trade is that of a combined manager, priest, policeman and advocate. Without an effective cadre network the insurgency loses the support of the villagers, without which the movement is doomed.

The American Concept of War

The American soldiers who arrived in Vietnam in 1965 brought with them a clear and deeply held institutional understanding of how to wage war. Characteristically, the American way of war required the orchestration of intensive firepower, advanced technology, and abundant matèriel in order to inflict maximum damage on the enemy. The goal was to dominate the battlefield to such an extent that the American forces would quickly break the enemy's will to resist and bring the conflict to a rapid conclusion. The origin of the US concept of conventional war lay in the American Civil War, and was reinforced by its experiences during the Second World War and Korean War. It was also the type of battle the United States planned to wage against the Soviet Union in Europe.

Confident and committed to their concept of war, the Americans did not make a distinction between the requirements for waging conventional and counter-insurgency wars. By contrast, British and Australian experience in counter-insurgency warfare highlighted the need for commanders to assign equal, if not greater, weight to a conflict's political dimensions instead of focusing solely on military considerations. Senior United States officers did not share this belief. The Chairman of the

Joint Chiefs of Staff, General Earle Wheeler, commented with complete self-assurance that, 'the essence of the problem in Vietnam is military.' When asked for his answer to the insurgency, the Commander of the United States Military Assistance Command Vietnam (COMUSMACV), General William Westmoreland, replied, 'firepower'.

In 1965 it was Westmoreland's responsibility to design, implement and oversee the American plan for the defeat of the VC. He was a devotee of the US concept of war, and his operational goal was to search out and destroy the enemy as quickly as possible. Westmoreland intended to direct a war of attrition and mobility in which he would break VC resistance by inflicting casualties at a rate greater than they could accept. Nor would the communists be able to hide. The Americans would use helicopters to swoop down on the enemy wherever they lay, and then rapidly redeploy to the next target. Westmoreland planned a campaign the intensity and speed of which the VC could not match. In the parlance of the day its aim was to 'find, fix and finish' the enemy, and to do it as quickly as possible.

Westmoreland's strategy was a thoroughly conventional approach to warfighting that incorporated American cultural values and made use of his force's strengths. However, it was also intellectually rigid and completely ignorant of the nature of insurgency warfare. MACV intended to transform the Vietnam campaign into a conventional-style war in which it would be able to bring to bear its great advantages over the enemy in firepower, technology and mass. Whether the VC would agree to this transformation and allow themselves to be annihilated, was not a point of concern for American planners.

Even had the Americans proceeded at a slower pace, and paid greater attention to the principles of counter-insurgency warfare, the realities of their concept of war made the winning of the local people's hearts and minds prohibitively difficult. The widespread and indiscriminate application of mass firepower, and a reliance on technology rather than personal contact, had severe consequences for the well-being of the local people. The effect of the American way of war on the population, however, was rarely a factor in the force's mantra of killing VC. In February 1967, for example, the American 1 Cavalry Division conducted an operation in Binh Dinh Province. During its three-month course, the division's ordnance expenditure included:

- 136,000 rounds of artillery
- 5,000 rounds of naval gun fire support
- 171 B-52 sorties
- 2,622 fighter bomber sorties

- 500,000 pounds of napalm
- 35,000 pounds of tear gas

The operation was considered a success since it netted 1,757 VC KIA. Yet it also displaced 12,000 villagers whose homes and farms 1 Cavalry Division had destroyed. It is not possible to determine how many of these villagers became recruits for the VC, but the American offensive probably did little to garner the support of Binh Dinh's peasants.

Handicapping American planning was MACV's inability to develop a methodology that documented the efficacy of its strategy of attrition. Possession of territory and the occupation of strategic points, both traditional indicators of success, were meaningless in the context of Vietnam. Instead, MACV turned to statistics. The most infamous of these was the body count: each dead VC brought the United States closer to victory.

General William Westmoreland (r) with the Commander of 1ATF Brigadier O. D. Jackson.
AWM CUN/66/0370/VN.

The reporting process became a self-fulfilling prophecy—and one that was not really representative of the course of the war. Moreover, the importance of submitting statistical increases encouraged commanders to expend matèriel without concern for the local people. It is not known how many non-VC were included in body count submissions, but the system rewarded the reporting of the highest number possible.

There was some opposition to the attrition strategy and the concept's inability to treat the conflict as a counter-insurgency operation. However, such opposition was aberrant. It lay outside the US Army's mainstream, and was unable to breach the institution's commitment to its way of war. The most vigorous alternate strategy was the United States Marines Combined Action Platoon Program. This program saw the forming of mixed Marine and Popular Force platoons. Each platoon occupied a village and provided its defence. The platoons remained in place for the duration and their members became familiar with the local people while gradually extending the safe zone around their location. This initiative did not have Westmoreland's approval, but the Marines were a separate service and MACV could not stop them from proceeding with this policy.

When the United States opted for military intervention in Vietnam, no one in Washington or Saigon considered the nature of the army that was to deploy, whether it was prepared for the conflict, or what it would do differently from the French. Instead, reliance on the army's concept was complete—a faith that the course of the war showed to be seriously misplaced. Setbacks resulted not in the concept's reconsideration, but in demands for more resources in order to increase its intensity. In the aftermath of defeat, General of the Army Omar Bradley summarised his force's performance in Vietnam as, 'the wrong place, at the wrong time, with the wrong army'.

The Australian Experience of Counter-Insurgency War

The Australians also entered the Vietnam War with a well-considered and inculcated concept of war. However, unlike that of the United States Army, the Australian Army's concept was specifically designed for the waging of counter-insurgency warfare against communist guerrillas in the jungles of South-East Asia. It derived from the army's recent experience in fighting Communist Terrorists during the Malayan Emergency. The Australian Army documented these experiences in doctrinal publications such as: *Ambush and Counter Ambush*; *Patrolling and Tracking*; and *The Division in Battle – Counter Revolutionary Warfare*, and incorporated these lessons into the curriculum of the Jungle Training Centre at Canungra. By the time of its intervention in Vietnam the army had an institutionally accepted doctrine of counter-insurgency which had been practised in exercises.

The Australian battalion group that arrived in Vietnam in 1965 had trained to fight as light infantry. Light infantry was a logical template for a force that lacked the manpower and resources to wage war on the scale of the United States. The battalion's skills lay in patrolling, ambushing and searching—all traditional areas of Australian excellence. The Australians also understood that progress was slow in counter-insurgency warfare; there would be no quick victory.

The American and Australian concepts of war contained points of conflict and contradiction that affected the conduct of operations, and which were never resolved during the conflict. The priority for MACV was rapid and decisive victory through search and destroy missions. For the Australians, search and destroy operations were not necessarily the most important of the available mix of mission types. Instead, cordon and search, interdiction, anti-logistic, political support, and civil action missions matched more closely the Australian understanding of how to achieve victory in an insurgency.

After his service in Vietnam, Brigadier S. G. Graham summarised the differences between the two allies. While in Vietnam he had attended a US briefing that had begun with the statement 'Our mission is to kill VC.' Graham believed that his mission was more complex. He described it as:

> to help to ensure the security of the main areas of population and resources of Phuoc Tuy and so enable the Government to restore law and order and get on with the job of developing the social, economical, and political life of the province.

While Australian commanders had great latitude, they still had to respond to American operational priorities. Hence, search and destroy missions were always a feature of Australian operations, even when their effectiveness was doubtful. The aftermath of most search and destroy missions amounted to tired troops and, at best, a few VC casualties and the destruction of a few abandoned bases. In fact, in many cases, sweeps of the jungle failed to locate any enemy at all.

In Vietnam medical evacuation was one of the more important roles for the helicopter. At secure LZs, dust off helicopters usually chose to land. Here an American chopper loads Australian casualties. AWM EKN/67/0147/VN.

As very much the junior partner in the alliance, the Australians had little ability to influence US strategy. The only opportunity to shape the nature of the war occurred at a conference in Honolulu from 30 March to 1 April 1965, prior to the commitment of combat forces. Leading the Australian contingent was the Chairman of the Chiefs of Staff Committee, Air Chief Marshal Frederick Scherger. At this point the United States had not clearly thought through fundamental issues that included the overall strategy and goal of military intervention, the required force mix, and the implications of the arrival of foreign forces in a national conflict. Scherger allowed Australia's opportunity to influence these choices to pass and, instead, the meeting focused on operational areas. The American concept remained unchallenged and it prevailed almost by default.

Portrait of Private Robert Schaeche of 11 Platoon 7 RAR.
'The Forward Scout' by Bruce Fletcher.
AWM ART40553.

Military Forces of the Republic of Vietnam

The final military forces with which the Australians had to contend were those of the Republic of Vietnam. These consisted of two main categories; the Army of the Republic of Vietnam (ARVN) and the Territorial Forces.

After the founding of South Vietnam, the United States made considerable efforts to build the ARVN into a conventional field force in its own image. By 1965 it was clear that this had failed: the ARVN did not have sufficient combat skill to trouble the VC in battle. Once US ground forces entered the conflict American Commanders lost interest in ARVN's further development. In effect, the South Vietnamese Army was no longer required because the defeat of the VC had become an American task.

The ARVN did contain some high quality units, but most of its troops were suited for little more than garrison duty. When Colonel, later Brigadier, O.D. Jackson toured Vietnam he observed that South Vietnamese troops typically remained dug in on hilltops behind wire from which they rarely ventured forth. The American Ambassador to South Vietnam and a former chairman of the Joint Chiefs of Staff, Maxwell Taylor, observed that 'we never really paid attention to the ARVN Army. We didn't give a damn about them.'

South Vietnam's Territorial Force divided into two sections: Popular Force and Regional Force units. Their task was to provide local security at the hamlet, village and district levels. The Territorial Force was not under ARVN command; being provincial—not national—forces they were under the control of the Province and District headquarters. While at the coalface of the insurgency, for most of the war the Territorial Force attracted little interest from MACV and received indifferent support from the government in Saigon. As a result, the units of the Territorial Force were poorly led and equipped, suffered from low morale, and often had been infiltrated by the VC. It was only late in the war that a concerted effort was made to improve the Territorial Force, but by that point it was too late.

Owen Machine Carbine (Australia) [Owen Gun]

Calibre:	9 mm
Action:	Blow-back
Length:	812 mm
Weight:	
5 kg (loaded)	
Muzzle Velocity:	
381 mps	
Magazine:	33 rounds
Rate of Fire:	600 rpm:
Effective Range:	
up to 100 m	

The locally designed and manufactured Owen Machine Carbine earned a reputation as one of the best submachine guns of the Second World War. It entered production in late 1942 and won favour with Australian troops fighting the Japanese in New Guinea. It was a tough, easy to handle weapon which stood up to the conditions of jungle warfare. Its simple interior design meant that it rarely jammed. However, by 1965 it was a tired weapon, and its lack of stopping power beyond minimum range resulted in its replacement with the American M16.

The Owen Machine Carbine. RAICM.

INTO BATTLE

Australia Goes to War

In early June 1965, Australian combat units arrived in Vietnam. The Australian presence in South Vietnam now consisted of three elements: a battalion group built around 1 RAR at Bien Hoa airfield; AAFV (Australian Army Force Vietnam) Headquarters in Saigon; and AATTV (Australian Army Training Team Vietnam) working in small parties scattered across the country. By September the contingent numbered nearly 1500 men. In addition, New Zealand deployed a field battery which served alongside the 1 RAR group, thereby reviving the Anzac tradition. At Bien Hoa the Australian force consisted of:

- 1 APC Troop (PWLH)
- 105 Field Battery
- 3 Field Troop
- 1 RAR
- 708 Signal Troop
- 105 Field Battery LAD (det)
- 161 (Indep) Recce Flight
- 1 Australian Logistic Support Company

When 1 RAR deployed, the Chief of the General Staff (CGS), Lieutenant-General John Wilton, issued a directive that placed AAFV under the operational control of MACV. Westmoreland in turn assigned 1 RAR to 173 Airborne Brigade (Separate), whose commander was Brigadier-General Ellis Williamson. Lieutenant-Colonel Ivan 'Lou' Brumfield's diggers became the brigade's third manoeuvre battalion. However, national command remained with Jackson as COMAAFV in Saigon, and he had the right to veto any operation that violated Australian national interests.

The Australian government's initial rules of engagement did not allow 1 RAR to deploy away from the general area of Bien Hoa without the approval of Army Headquarters in Canberra. There was some confusion over the geographical interpretation of this restriction, and MACV initially limited the Australians to the defence of the airfield, an inappropriate use of a well-trained battalion. Moreover, when restricted to a garrison role the battalion did not face the same risks as the Americans, which minimised Australia's role in the alliance with the United States and negated one of the government's prime rationales for the deployment.

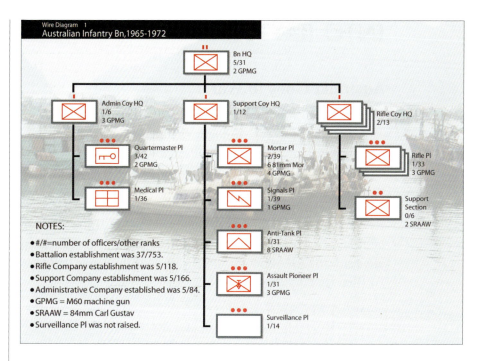

Wire Diagram 1
Australian Infantry Bn, 1965-1972

Bn HQ
5/31
2 GPMG

Admin Coy HQ
1/6
3 GPMG

Support Coy HQ
1/12

Rifle Coy HQ
2/13

Quartermaster Pl
3/42
2 GPMG

Mortar Pl
2/39
6 81mm Mor
4 GPMG

Rifle Pl
1/33
3 GPMG

Medical Pl
1/36

Signals Pl
1/39
1 GPMG

Support
Section
0/6
2 SRAAW

Anti-Tank Pl
1/31
8 SRAAW

Assault Pioneer Pl
1/31
3 GPMG

Surveillance Pl
1/14

NOTES:

- #/#=number of officers/other ranks
- Battalion establishment was 37/753.
- Rifle Company establishment was 5/118.
- Support Company establishment was 5/166.
- Administrative Company established was 5/84.
- GPMG = M60 machine gun
- SRAAW = 84mm Carl Gustav
- Surveillance Pl was not raised.

Wire Diagram 1 illustrates the organisation of the Australian standard infantry battalion in the era of the Vietnam War. In addition to the listed support weapons the infantry's standard weapons were: Owen or F1 sub-machine guns (replaced by M16), L1A1 Rifle, M26 grenade, M72 rocket launcher and M79 grenade projector.
Mark Wahlert.

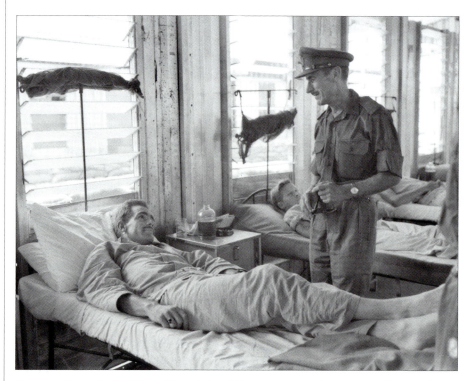

Lieutenant-General John Wilton visits an injured digger, Corporal Brian Basset, at the Australian hospital in Vung Tau.
AWM CRO/68/0257/VN

By September, however, high-level discussions between Wilton and Westmoreland clarified 1 RAR's area of operations and extended it to include the entire III Corps tactical zone. This remained Australia's service zone for the rest of the war, with the exception of the AATTV which continued to operate anywhere in South Vietnam.

Australian and American Operational Styles

While relations between the Australian and American soldiers were friendly and each earned the other's respect, combat experience exposed the dramatic differences that underpinned their concepts of war and operational procedures. One of the most significant contrasts was the function of time. The 1 RAR operations officer, Major John Essex-Clark, remembered that at his first meeting with Williamson the American commented that 'the war will be won in few months, once the Viet Cong feel the firepower of the Brigade.' Essex-Clark, however, recognised that the insurgency's defeat would take longer.

Once away from Bien Hoa the different expectations of the conflict's duration became readily apparent. American patrols received vast areas to clear, moved towards objectives by a direct path, and stuck to time-tables set by base-bound staff officers. An Australian patrol, by contrast, searched the jungle at a much slower pace than the Americans and followed a serendipitous route dictated by a combination of terrain and enemy signs. Seen from the air the respective patrols of the two allies moved so differently that on several occasions the Americans mistook the Australians for VC.

Compared to the diggers, the Yanks made extravagant claims of having cleared great tracts of land. Yet their rapid march and telegraphed route offered the VC opportunities to slip away whenever they wished. Because 1 RAR's men did not simply traverse the ground but sought to control it, land declared clean of VC by the Australians came with a higher degree of certainty.

On operations, Americans displayed a cockiness which Australians neither understood nor desired to emulate. In the bush the airborne soldiers invited contact with the VC by talking, smoking, firing their weapons, retaining brightly coloured patches on their uniforms, marching in columns, preferably along a track, and receiving resupply from helicopters. The Australians were the opposite. They moved stealthily, patrolling slowly and silently, fanning out in sections, refusing to walk on tracks, and avoiding helicopters until it was pick-up time. One Australian observer declared, 'keep those bloody choppers away from us – they give away our positions.'

Even in their bases the Americans continued to display a lack of caution where the VC were concerned. In the Bien Hoa compound at night the American units on either side of 1 RAR left electric lights on and routinely illuminated the approaches to their position with flares. Watching VC would have seen a mass of lights with a small black patch—the Australians—in the middle. The VC regularly mortared the American sectors of the base but left the Australian area alone.

'Chopper Lift-out', Ken McFadyen. Oil on Canvas. AWM ART40746.
The painting shows Australian troops boarding a Huey of 9 Squadron RAAF.

The American soldiers were neither slack nor poorly trained. Rather they were confident, elite warriors who possessed a gung-ho attitude that was backed up with a scale of weaponry the magnitude of which was beyond anything the Australians had previously experienced. American units taunted the VC to 'have a go', and in doing so accepted casualties as the price of having the opportunity to bring their firepower to bear.

The Australians did not have the depth of reserves that the Americans enjoyed. 1 RAR had no option but to husband its manpower because the Army could not replace it if the VC destroyed the unit. Thus the Australians adopted a more cautious approach to the enemy. Their message was, 'you will never know exactly where we are, but we will find you and kill you.'

Helicopter UH-1H, Iroquois 'Huey' (USA)	
Crew:	4
Passengers:	7
Length:	
17.4 m (with rotors)	
Width:	2.6 m
Height:	4.4 m
Engine:	
Lycoming T53-L-9 or 11 turboshaft, 1,400 SHP	
Max Speed:	204 kph
Range:	512 km
Service Ceiling:	4300 m
Armament:	
RAAF 'Bushranger' gunship carried: 2 x 7.62mm M134 Mini-guns; 2 x 2.75in Folding Fin Rocket Pods of 7 rockets each; and 4 x 7.62mm M60 GPMG (in 2 dual mounts)	

The Bell UH1 helicopter, popularly known as the 'Huey', is synonymous with the Vietnam War. It was used by 1 ATF to transport troops, equipment, and supplies, and evacuate casualties, and provide fire support to troops on the ground. Various nicknames were given to the 'Huey' in Vietnam, depending on its role. For example, 'Hogs' were gunships, 'Slicks' were troop transports, and a 'dust-off' was a medical evacuation. Up to 1967 the RAAF had flown the UH-1B version which had lesser capabilities and armament than the H model. In Vietnam 9 Squadron, RAAF, operated the 'Huey', which was eventually replaced in the Australian Army by the UH60 Blackhawk.

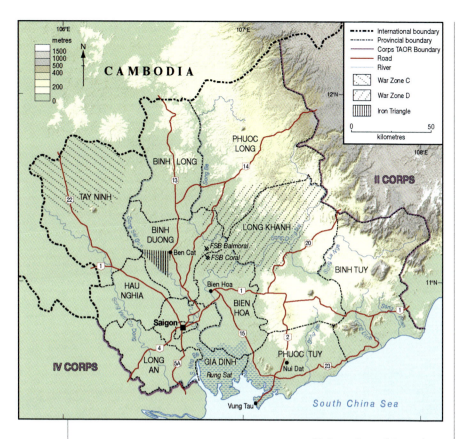

III Corps Area of Operations.
Anthony Bright.

The Australian 'go slow' approach, however, did gain their ally's respect. One American battalion commander called the Australians 'quiet hunters – patient, thorough, trying to out think the Viet Cong.' He continued, 'I would not have liked to operate at night and know there was a chance of ending up in an Aussie ambush.' In another example, 1 Infantry Division (US) specifically requested 1 RAR's assistance during Operation *Abilene*. Australian excellence at patrolling had become common knowledge, and the divisional commander wanted 1 RAR, not an American battalion, to protect his fire support and logistic bases.

Even language posed difficulties for the two allies. The Australians had to learn a host of Yank expressions in order to avoid confusion, especially during radio transmissions. A 'slick', for example, was a Huey transport helicopter and a 'dust-off' was a medical evacuation. When 1 RAR arrived in Vietnam its signallers used the Able Baker Charlie Dog phonetic code for radio procedures, but had to adapt to the prevailing American usage—Alpha Bravo Charlie Delta. The language problem was so serious that when Jackson visited Williamson's headquarters for the first time he found an Australian soldier outside the airborne brigade commander's tent. When asked what he was doing the soldier replied, 'Sir, I'm the interpreter.' Brumfield had assigned him to the Americans.

The area of American activity that drew the greatest wonder and perplexity from the Australians was the employment of helicopters. High aerial mobility was 173rd's *raison d'etre*. According to its advocates, helicopter aviation was the coming arm in the art of war. Between the Korean and Vietnam wars the United States Army intensely debated the role of tactical aviation on the battlefield. They did not see the helicopter as a counter-insurgency weapon. Instead its advocates wanted to exploit its manoeuvre potential on a nuclear battlefield against the Soviet Union. 173 Airborne Brigade (Separate) was one of the first formations raised for this purpose, and was 'light' only in the sense that it was not armoured.

An Australian 105 mm L5 Pack Howitzer. This gun was to be replaced by the more robust American M2A2.
AWM P01612.003.

An American Hueycobra. The Americans made prodigious use of aerial firepower.
AWM P01980.015.

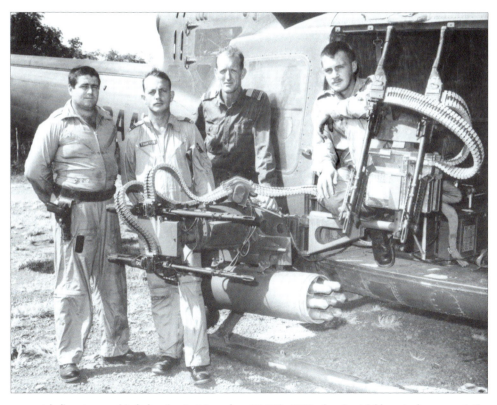

A helicopter gunship belonging to 9 Squadron RAAF in 1968, showing trial layout of armament. The helicopter is armed with a XM 157 airborne rocket pod containing seven 2.75 inch rockets, twin side-mounted M60 machine-guns and twin door-mounted M60 machine-guns.
AWM P01999.001.

Essex-Clark described a typical American helicopter insertion. The sequence was:

1. F-100 Super Sabres bomb edge of landing zone;
2. A1-E Skyraiders drop Napalm;
3. helicopter gunships strafe area with machine-gun and rocket fire;
4. artillery pounds the landing zone; and finally
5. a phosphorus smoke round announces end of prep fire and the transport helicopters begin their descent.

He concluded that a helicopter insertion accomplished little. At best it saved on walking and the troops arrived fresh at the insertion point. However, the accompanying noise and firepower display revealed the Americans' planned tactical area of responsibility (TAOR), and thereby surrendered the initiative, allowing the VC either to slip away or set an ambush as they desired.

Having experienced them first hand, Essex-Clark left a vivid recollection of participating in an American helicopter-borne insertion. He wrote:

> an air-mobile assault is a roller-coaster helicopter ride accompanied by a screeching Wagner and a thundering Guy Fawkes. It is madness, and the surrealism makes me laugh with incredulity. It is adventure, it is excitement, but it is utter fantasyland.

He concluded, 'what on earth are the VC thinking as they slip away from all this bother?'

Lesson 2

Even closely related military organisations have peculiar national characteristics that can impede operational effectiveness. These distinctions must be identified and overcome if the members of a coalition are to work together seamlessly.

Into Battle

Williamson allowed 1 RAR two weeks to acclimatise to Vietnam, after which it was to be available for operations. During its tour the battalion participated in numerous operations, mostly search and destroy. These operations did more than just highlight differences in American and Australian characteristics; they also hinted at deeper problems in each nation's concept of war.

By mid-1965 the VC had commenced phase three operations and controlled much of the countryside. If the United States was to prevent the fall of the South it had to halt the enemy's offensive. This played to the American strengths, but while firepower and mobility accounted for many VC, the technique lacked subtlety. It also did not acknowledge that the VC response to American success would be to revert to phase two operations, against which sound counter-insurgency principles were even more essential if the United States was to reap the political benefit of its battlefield victories.

While the Australians did not see long-term benefit in the American concept, the diggers certainly appreciated their ally's capabilities when needed. Vietnam was not Malaya and the VC were far better equipped and organised than the small bands of insurgents the Australians had faced during the Emergency. On more than one occasion, during Operation *Hump* for example, firepower was instrumental in breaking up VC concentrations. Again, 1 RAR would have been in serious trouble if not for the fire and aerial support it received during Operation *Crimp*.

Stealthy patrolling was an effective way of locating the enemy and controlling the jungle, but if battle did join, the rapid provision of firepower gave the American and Australian soldiers a crucial advantage. A key question, therefore, was whether the Americans and Australians should have sought battle in the first place, instead of conducting the conflict more according to counter-insurgency principles. This was not an option in 1965 once the VC entered phase three. However, having stabilised the situation and prevented the VC from toppling the government of Vietnam (GVN), the allies had the opportunity to reconsider their methods. Yet the Americans left their concept unquestioned. They continued to emphasise search and destroy operations and, in so doing, encouraged a stalemate that benefited the more patient communists. There was a pressing need for the Americans to seek alternative options, such as to target the VC's cadre and political organisation. But this was beyond the scope of American warfighting doctrine.

1 RAR on Operations

Search and destroy was the most common operation in which 1 RAR participated. A typical example was Operation *Crimp* which took place over the period 8 to 14 January 1966 in the Ho Bo Woods, a long-established VC sanctuary near the 'Iron Triangle'. The target was an enemy headquarters, the Saigon-Cholon-Gia Special Sector Committee which was known to be in the area.

Lesson 3

The effort committed to reconnaissance is rarely wasted. However, commanders must always take care to avoid alerting the enemy to a pending operation.

A few days before insertion, Essex-Clark conducted a single flypast at 1500 feet over the target. He had acquired the habit of reconnoitring the landing zone and taking photos of the area with a Polaroid camera that he had purchased. He allowed himself only a single flypast in order not to reveal his interest to the enemy.

In this instance the resulting pictures concerned Essex-Clark sufficiently that he took them to 1 RAR's new commander, Lieutenant-Colonel Alex Preece. They revealed virtually no leaves under the rubber trees that surrounded the landing zone, as well as oddly placed drainage ditches leading off from a road. While the images did not show clear proof of enemy activity they did reveal unnatural disturbances for which the most likely explanation was VC intervention. Essex-Clark deduced that it was soil from newly dug positions that had covered the normal pattern of leaf fall, and that the drainage ditches were tunnels. From these positions the enemy had excellent fields of fire over an open area called the 'Cabbage Patch', the piece of ground which planners had selected as the Australians' landing zone. After a heated exchange at brigade headquarters the planners agreed to shift 1 RAR's landing zone 200 metres, still uncomfortably near the Cabbage Patch, but out of the immediate line of fire of the strange marks Essex-Clark had observed.

A sapper of 3 Field Troop emerges from a VC tunnel during Operation *Crimp*.
AWM KEL/66/0021/VN.

Some of the enemy weapons recovered by 1 RAR during Operation *Crimp*.
AWM P01595.071.

Essex-Clark's fly-over proved fortuitous. Even with the shift, 1 RAR assaulted a hot landing zone. Sweeping the Cabbage Patch was a battery of 12.7 mm anti-aircraft (AA) guns, and VC fire positions riddled the area. The Cabbage Patch sat above a major tunnel system that housed the enemy's headquarters and, for this reason, was heavily defended. Throughout the day VC popped up, fired, and disappeared back underground from within the Australian perimeter. During the night enemy squads shifted positions while underneath the Australians the ground was alive with noises and the sounds of VC talking. In C Company's area, Private Ray Payne fired his machine-gun at a group of VC that had advanced towards him down a trench. He held his fire as a patrol was expected back along the same route. At a range of just a few centimetres, the first VC's chest exploded from the impact while behind him others fell to the ground wounded.

The next morning sappers from 3 Field Troop started to explore the tunnels. Over the next few days they discovered an underground city of living, working and storage chambers, and linking tunnels that ran for kilometres. This was a part of what would become known as the Cu Chi Tunnel Complex. In the time allowed the sappers penetrated just a fraction of the network. They pulled out piles of weapons, supplies and documents, among them an outline of the regional headquarters and a list of VC agents in Saigon. The operation's cost to the Australians was 8 KIA and 29 wounded in action (WIA).

Operation *Crimp* produced two important intelligence lessons. It confirmed the necessity for careful preparation and the value of examining the area of operations in advance. Second, the operation underscored the importance of searching the enemy's underground strongholds. The documents the Australians recovered provided MACV with a detailed outline of the VC organisation around Saigon.

Prior to Operation *Crimp* the Americans had avoided venturing underground. Instead they simply blew in the tunnels. Their priority was to kill VC not engage in subterranean exploration. Following Operation *Crimp*, Williamson ordered his paratroopers to go below.

Private Russell Wiseman of 7 RAR tapes his grenade before moving out on an ambush. This photo was taken in 1971 and illustrates that the policy of lever taping begun by 1 RAR lasted until the end of the conflict.
AWM CUN/71/0054/VN.

Operation *New Life*

Operation *New Life* was one of the few non-search and destroy missions in which 1 RAR participated. It was a rice denial operation set in the La Nga Valley near Vo Dat, about 80 kilometres north-east of Bien Hoa. The La Nga Valley, one of South Vietnam's grain baskets, was under VC domination. The operation lasted from 21 November to 16 December 1965.

1 RAR deployed into Vo Dat and was given responsibility for a 90-square-kilometre area of operations centred on the village of Duc Hanh. The diggers' instructions were to clear their sector of VC in order to allow the GVN to bring in the harvest and restore control over the villagers. The Americans left the planning to the battalion which, at this time, was under the temporary command of Major Mal Lander.

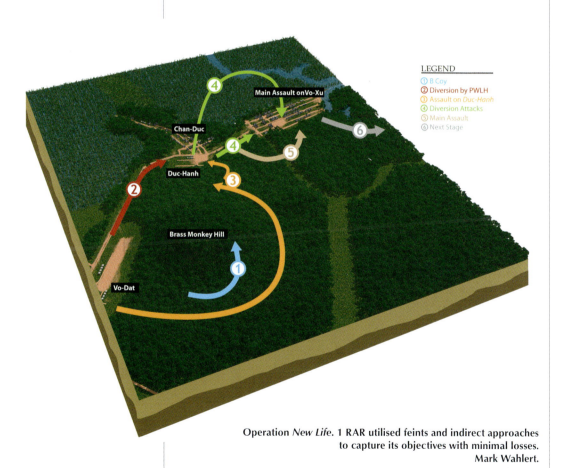

LEGEND
① B Coy
② Diversion by PWLH
③ Assault on *Duc-Hanh*
④ Diversion Attacks
⑤ Main Assault
⑥ Next Stage

Operation *New Life*. 1 RAR utilised feints and indirect approaches to capture its objectives with minimal losses.
Mark Wahlert.

The GVN had fortified Duc Hanh before its loss to the VC. Its defences consisted of a dry moat and a wire barrier with mines on the likely approach routes. The valley's main road ran straight through the village, passing through stout wooden gates at each end. Within the village the VC had dug a network of trenches. Intelligence reports estimated the enemy's garrison at about 90.

Lander decided on a plan in which deception played a key part. On 22 November the battalion moved out of Vo Dat and into the jungle. As a precaution Lander had B Company scale a feature known as the 'Brass Monkey' to deny the VC the high ground for observation. On the night of 23/24 November, the battalion secretly leaguered near Duc Hanh, in position to assault the next day.

At first light the armoured personnel carriers (APCs) of the Prince of Wales Light Horse (PWLH) thundered down the road from Vo Dat towards Duc Hanh. At the same time the New Zealand gunners bombarded the western side of the village while helicopter gunships buzzed above. Having learned that noise and explosions preceded an attack, the VC took up defensive positions along the village's western edge.

A party of soldiers from C Company 1 RAR prepare to search a house during Operation *New Life*.
AWM SHA/65/0302/VN.

Lander, however, had correctly anticipated the enemy's reaction to his feint. Instead of attacking from the west, he planned to assault Duc Hanh from the east, emerging from the jungle. He tasked D Company, with the assault pioneers, to break into the village, while B and C Companies set up a screen in the jungle line along its eastern side. A Company remained in reserve.

As the VC moved so did D Company. The assault pioneers quickly cleared paths through the wire and minefield, and the diggers broke into the village. The VC soon realised they had been tricked, however, and the Australians came under fire. A running firefight developed as D Company's commander, Captain Peter Rothwell, urged his platoons forward to secure the village before the VC had time to reorganise its defence. Sections divided into fire and movement teams, supporting one another as they advanced. If fired upon from a building, one team pinned the enemy while the other closed and silenced them with grenades.

The impetus of the attack took the Australians into the centre of Duc Hanh, from which they observed the VC attempting to establish a new position on the village's northern side. The commander of the right-most platoon, Second Lieutenant Jim Bourke, called up the New Zealand battery and directed shells onto the VC. The enemy broke and withdrew. It had been a good day for the battalion. Suffering no casualties themselves, they had cleared Duc Hanh and inflicted on their enemy 15 KIA, 7 taken as prisoners of war (POW) and many more wounded.

The Australians' next targets were the villages of Chan Duc and Vo Xu. The latter they captured after again employing a feint, this time a mock helicopter assault. Operation *New Life*'s success, however, was short-lived. The ARVN took over the valley's protection but could not hold it. La Nga was soon once again under VC control.

THE SITUATION IN PHUOC TUY

Phuoc Tuy: A VC Stronghold

Soon after 1 RAR's deployment to Bien Hoa, Wilton began to explore the battalion group's expansion to a task force. A larger contingent had several benefits. These included:

- allowing Australia to field a separate force, resulting in greater national recognition;

- allowing the task force greater military independence;

- allowing units to fight in their own style rather than using American tactics; and

- providing additional combat forces to the hard-pressed MACV.

The CGS had another rationale. In Korea he had witnessed first hand the American tendency to slog it out with the enemy and their willingness to accept casualties at a level greater than he was prepared to tolerate. The airborne brigade to which 1 RAR had been attached displayed a 'gung ho' attitude that worried Wilton. He believed a degree of separation from the Americans would allow the Australians to fight according to their own techniques and help shield them from unnecessary casualties. On 8 March 1966 the government confirmed the deployment's expansion, which was to be known as 1 Australian Task Force (1 ATF).

The task force's operational restrictions were similar to those under which 1 RAR operated. Wilton and Westmoreland agreed that 1 ATF would have four tasks, namely:

1. secure and dominate its TAOR in Phuoc Tuy;
2. conduct operations to secure Route 15;
3. conduct other operations in Phuoc Tuy as needed; and
4. conduct operations anywhere in the III Corps Tactical Zone as required, as well as in the province of Binh Thuan in II Corps Tactical Zone.

The generals placed 1 ATF under the operational control of the American HQ II Field Force Vietnam (FFV).

In selecting the task force's location Wilton adopted several criteria. He determined that the location:

- should be an area of significant enemy activity;
- should not lie near the Cambodian and Laotian borders or the de-militarised zone (DMZ);

- should have access to the sea; and
- shall be a distinct area of a size suitable for the task force.

Of the several regions considered, Phuoc Tuy Province, 40 miles east of Saigon, met the criteria most closely. The port of Vung Tau was nearby and it was well suited to serve as the task force's entry point and logistic base. In addition, if the deployment went badly, Vung Tau would become its evacuation point.

Phuoc Tuy was VC territory. Virtually all of the province's 100,000 people lived under communist control and the GVN's mandate barely extended into the rice paddies that surrounded Ba Ria, the provincial capital. South Vietnamese forces traversed Route 15—the main link between Ba Ria and Saigon—at their peril and only under heavy escort. The province's other roads were even more dangerous.

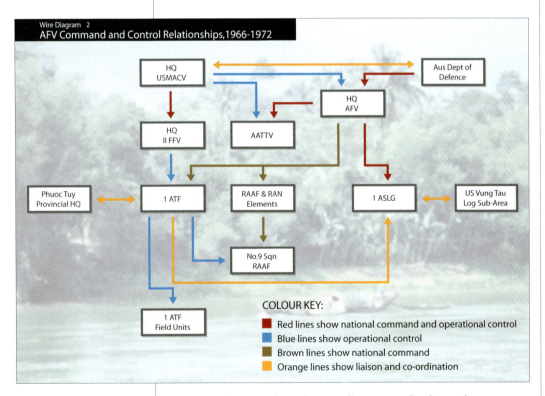

Wire Diagram 2
AFV Command and Control Relationships,1966-1972

COLOUR KEY:
- Red lines show national command and operational control
- Blue lines show operational control
- Brown lines show national command
- Orange lines show liaison and co-ordination

Wire Diagram 2 shows the Australian command and control arrangements following the arrival of the task force in 1966. It illustrates the multiple chains of command and relationships among and between Australian and MACV entities. Mark Wahlert.

Detail of a M16 fitted with a 20 round magazine. A 30 round magazine is also shown. RAICM.

Armalite, AR15 (M16) Rifle (USA)

Calibre: 5.56 mm
Operation:
Gas operation, magazine fed, selective fire – semi automatic and automatic fire
Length: 980 mm
Weight:
3.3 kg (loaded)
Muzzle velocity:
991 m/sec
Magazine:
20/30 rounds
Rate of fire: 800 rpm
Effective range: 300 m

The M16 rifle was the standard issue for US infantrymen in Vietnam. When the Australian Army deployed to Vietnam its section-level automatic weapons were the Owen Gun and the F1 sub-machine-gun. Both proved inadequate and the Australians adopted the M16 instead. It fired a 5.56mm bullet at a rate of 750–900 rounds per minute on automatic setting, or as fast as a soldier could pull the trigger on semi-automatic. Before a redesign in 1966, the M16s responded poorly to wet, dirty field conditions, and often jammed during combat. M16 cartridges came in 20 or 30-round 'clips', which could be quickly popped in and out of the rifle's loading port during firefights. Although the clips added weight to the soldier's gear, the danger of running out of ammunition during a firefight caused many 'grunts' to carry as many clips as they could stand when they went into the field.

Private Ken Answer of 5 RAR on patrol with an M16 rifle. Slung over his left shoulder is an M79 grenade launcher.
AWM COM/69/0428/VN.

Since the war with the French the VC had built an extensive cadre and political organisation that penetrated every village and town in Phuoc Tuy. On the province's periphery, in its mountainous and jungle-clad terrain, the communists had established base areas from which main force units operated. The VC's main bases were hidden in the Long Hai Hills in the south, the May Tao Mountains in the north-east, the Nui Dinh and Nui Thi Vai Hills overlooking Route 15, and the Hat Dich area that straddled the western border.

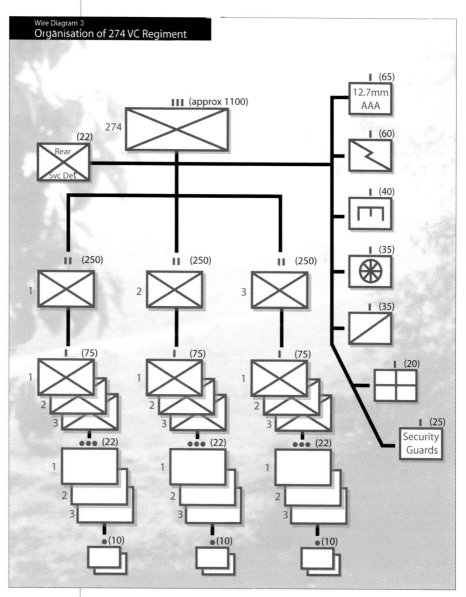

Wire Diagram 3
Organisation of 274 VC Regiment

Wire Diagram 3 illustrates the structure and establishment of *274 VC Regiment*. It shows that a VC regiment was a balanced force and the approximate equivalent of an Australian battalion group.
Mark Wahlert.

The communists maintained a hierarchy of military units in the province. The main force formation was *5 VC Division HQ* with its associated *274* and *275 VC Regiments*, each comprising three battalions and divisional support units. The regional units were the *D445 Provincial Mobile Battalion*, whose main base was the Long Hai Hills, and five district companies. At the local level most villages supported a guerrilla platoon. In total, Phuoc Tuy contained over 5,000 insurgents. Wire diagram 3 illustrates the organisation of *274 VC Regiment*.

Commanding the Australian Commitment

The expansion of Australia's commitment also necessitated modifications to its command and control arrangements. This was due to the increase of the ground deployment to a task force size, as well as the addition of force elements of the Royal Australian Air Force (RAAF), and later the Royal Australian Navy (RAN).

In April 1966, Major General K. Mackay arrived in Saigon to become the commander of HQ Australian Force Vietnam (AFV). In effect, this was the successor to HQ AAFV, the organisation which Jackson had led, and their functions would be similar. Jackson in turn moved to Nui Dat and took command of 1 ATF. Since Australia's commitment to Vietnam was now tri-service, HQ AFV was a joint environment, although the Army's presence was dominant.

The COMAFV was responsible for ensuring that the activities of 1 ATF and the other Australian elements in Vietnam adhered to the national interest as directed by the Australian government from Canberra. He did not command any field elements; 1 ATF, for example, was under the operational control of the US commander of Headquarters II Field Force Vietnam. Instead, the COMAFV possessed what is now termed 'the red card' and he could veto any operational task assigned to Australian forces. HQ AFV also exercised technical control. The COMAFV's staff contained corps representatives who provided technical oversight in matters pertaining to their specialities.

There was some debate over which service should provide the COMAFV. However, as the Vietnam War was largely a ground operation the Australian Army successfully argued that it should hold the senior position. At the RAAF's insistence the deputy commander position was given to an air commodore. This arrangement was reviewed the following year and the pattern of an army commander and a RAAF deputy was confirmed. A RAN presence at HQ AFV did not occur until 1967 with the opening of a Naval Staff Office. This was because it was not until then that the navy maintained an ongoing presence in the Vietnam theatre. The RAN's commitment consisted of a ship serving on the Gunline, as well as, ashore, a helicopter detachment of the Fleet Air Arm and divers of CDT3.

TABLE 1
Australian Force Vietnam Commanders

Commander	Commencement of Appointment
Major General K. Mackay	17 April 1966
Major General D. Vincent	31 January 1967
Major General A. L. MacDonald	30 January 1968
Major General R. A. Hay	1 February 1969
Major General C. A. E. Fraser	5 March 1970
Major General D. S. Dunstan	6 March 1971

The joint nature of HQ AFV did create some administrative problems. At that time Australia did not have a joint command mechanism and instead relied on a committee called the Chiefs of Staff Committee to coordinate the actions of the three services. For much of the conflict Wilton was the Chairman of the Chiefs of Staff Committee, but he had no statutory authority over any of the services. Instead, he issued directives to the COMAFV with the agreement of the service chiefs. In return, the COMAFV reported to the Chairman of the Chiefs of Staff Committee on joint matters, but on solely army matters he communicated to the Chief of the General Staff. The senior RAN and RAAF officer at HQ AFV also filled the role of service component commanders and reported up their respective chains of command on matters pertaining exclusively to their services.

Wire Diagram 2 outlines Australia's revised command and control relationships after the raising of HQ AFV and 1 ATF.

The Development of 1 ATF

The decision to deploy a task force to Phuoc Tuy saw a major expansion in Australia's commitment and resulted in the Commonwealth's largest overseas deployment since the Second World War. When first raised, the task force's major units consisted of:

- HQ 1 ATF
- 1 Armoured Personnel Carrier Squadron
- 1 Field Regiment (two Australian and one New Zealand batteries)
- 1 Field Squadron
- 21 Engineer Support Troop
- 103 Signal Squadron
- 5 RAR
- 6 RAR
- 3 Special Air Service Squadron
- 161 (Indep) Recce Flight
- detachment 1 Division Intelligence Unit

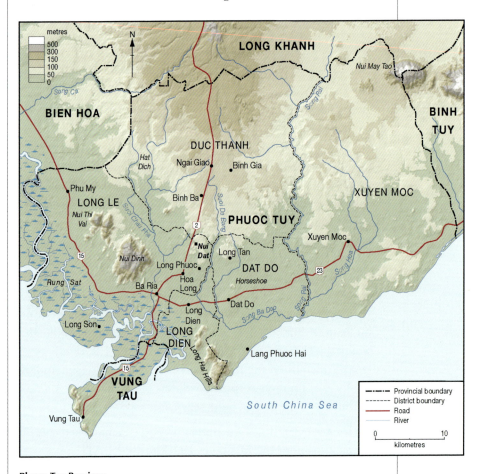

Phuoc Tuy Province.
Anthony Bright.

In addition, MACV provided 1 ATF with further resources. The most important were signallers and liaison officers who linked the task force to HQ II FFV and other United States headquarters. On Nui Dat's establishment, for example, was a United States Army Aviation officer through whom the Australians accessed American helicopters. Since 1 ATF did not include any heavy guns, the Americans lent the Australians a battery of six 155 mm self-propelled howitzers.

In 1968 the task force underwent a critically needed major expansion. The arrival of a third infantry battalion eased the workload on the task force's overburdened infantry and gave the Australian commander the ability to undertake a greater range of operations. The other significant reinforcement was two troops of Centurion tanks from C Squadron, 1 Armoured Regiment. Subsequent arrivals brought the squadron up to full strength of 26 vehicles including two dozer and two bridgelayer tanks.

TABLE 2
1 ATF Commanders

Commander	Commencement of Appointment
Brigadier O. D. Jackson	1 April 1966
Brigadier S. C. Graham	7 January 1967
Brigadier R. L. Hughes	20 October 1967
Brigadier C. M. I. Pearson	20 October 1968
Brigadier S. P. Weir	1 September 1969
Brigadier W. G. Henderson	1 June 1970
Brigadier B. A. McDonald	28 February 1971

Private John Sharp of 1 RAR mans his M60 machine-gun. The ammo belt's tendency to pick up leaf litter made the weapon susceptible to jamming. AWM ERR/68/0680/VN.

Close-up of the M60's feed mechanism. RAICM.

General Purpose Machine-Gun (GPMG) M60 (USA)

Calibre:
7.62 mm NATO
Action: Gas
Length: 1105 mm
Weight:
10.5 kg (on bi-pod)
Muzzle velocity:
853 m/sec
Feeding: belt
Rate of fire: 550 rpm
Effective range: 500 m

The General Purpose Machine-Gun (GPMG) M60 was designed in the late 1940s and borrowed heavily from German weaponry. It was the standard infantry section machine-gun for Australian troops in Vietnam. The M60 was gas-operated and belt-fed, and featured an interchangeable barrel and integral folding bipod. It could also be fired from tripod and vehicle mounts. It had some drawbacks: the bipods and the gas chamber were permanently attached to the barrel, so quick replacement of the hot barrel in battle conditions was awkward. The absence of a gas regulator meant that the weapon often continued to fire after the gunner released the trigger. The weapon also had a jamming problem as the belt dragged leaf litter into the feed mechanism. Home-grown modifications included an ammunition drum and running the belts through inner tubes. The most effective solution was to break the belt into short lengths that minimised contact with the ground. In the 1990s the Australian Army replaced the M60 with the F89 Minimi LSW.

Australia based its counter-insurgency doctrine around the capabilities of light infantry. On the surface, armour was the antithesis of such a role, and there were questions within the army on whether the benefits of deploying armour outweighed their considerable support and maintenance liabilities. The COMAFV of the time, Major-General D. Vincent, argued in their favour, observing that they would enhance 1 ATF's mobility and firepower. He also pointed out that tanks, simply by their presence, would raise the status of the Australian army in the eyes of the United States. The importance of mobile firepower in battle against VC main force units could not be denied.

Between its raising in 1966 and its disbandment in 1972 1 ATF had seven commanders (listed in Table 2).

Supporting 1 ATF was 1 ALSG (Australian Logistic Support Group) at Vung Tau. Its organisation comprised engineer, transport, ordnance, medical and service corps units, including:

- HQ 1 ALSG
- 17 Construction Squadron
- detachment 32 Small Ships Squadron
- 87 Transport Platoon
- 21 Supply Platoon
- detachment 176 Air Dispatch Company
- 2 Field Ambulance
- 101 Field Workshop
- detachment 1 Division Postal Unit
- 1 Australian Rest and Convalescence Centre

The New Zealand contribution to South Vietnam also increased after the raising of 1 ATF. In addition to its howitzer battery, New Zealand provided either one or two companies of infantry, depending on the rotation. These became an Australian battalion's 'V' and/or 'W' company. In 1969 New Zealand further expanded its role in Phuoc Tuy with the addition of a Special Air Service Troop.

The Decision for Nui Dat

Having decided on Phuoc Tuy, the Australians next needed to select a location for their base. There were only three viable options: Ba Ria—the capital; Vung Tau—the entry port; and a location to be selected in the province's central region. Wilton quickly eliminated Ba Ria as he wanted to maintain a degree of separation between the Australians and the local population. He also discounted Vung Tau because of its distance from the enemy's strongholds. What Wilton wanted was a site in the middle of the province away from main population centres but close to the VC's base areas. He sought to position the task force between the VC and the people so that Australian patrols could separate the guerrillas from the villagers. Wilton's choice was Nui Dat in the heart of the province and in the middle of VC country.

Some officers, for example Wilton's successor as CGS Major-General Thomas Daly, believed the selection of Nui Dat was a mistake. Since Australia had already decided to establish a base at Vung Tau they argued that 1 ATF should collocate with its support organisation. This way Australia would need to maintain just one base and thereby make considerable savings in resources and manpower.

However, Nui Dat best met 1 ATF's operational requirements, and from it the Australians were well placed to antagonise enemy forces, disrupt their logistics, and free the villages from the grasp of the insurgents.

Off Limits—Phuoc Tuy's Villages

The Australians never owned Phuoc Tuy; rather they shared responsibility for its defence with the GVN, ARVN and Territorial Forces, and the Americans. In reality the province contained three TAORs. The Territorial Force units had responsibility for the close protection of the people and guarded Phuoc Tuy's towns and villages. The countryside was the responsibility of the Australians. In addition, American formations based in the adjoining provinces frequently operated in Phuoc Tuy, and when this happened II FFV usually requested 1 ATF's assistance. The province's TAORs could and did overlap both geographically and operationally.

The Australians did not hold South Vietnamese provincial troops in high regard. A former CGS, Lieutenant-General Peter Gration, described them as 'incompetent and lacking in motivation', summing them up as 'inept, with no stomach for the fight'. The GVN Province Chief commanded 17 Regional Force Companies, 47 Popular Force Platoons, and a small regular force infantry battalion. All had low combat qualities and they rarely left their compounds.

Rifle, L1A1 SLR FN FAL (Belgium)

Calibre:
7.62 mm NATO
Operation:
Gas operation, magazine fed, semi automatic fire
Length: 1,137 mm
Weight: 5 kg (loaded)
Muzzle velocity: 823 m/sec
Magazine: 20 rounds
Rate of fire:
up to 20 aimed shots per minute
Effective range: 300 m

The 7.62 mm L1A1 SLR was an Australian version of the Belgian FN (*Fabrique Nationale*) FAL (*Fusil Automatique Leger*—Light Automatic Rifle). It was a very successful military rifle and was adopted by numerous armies. The L1A1 proved a reliable, robust and effective semi-automatic weapon. In Vietnam, it was the standard personal weapon of the Australian soldier. Australia manufactured the L1A1 under licence at the Lithgow Small Arms Factory.

Private Nicholas Andropof carries the Australian L1A1 rifle and an American M72. Although designed as an anti-armour weapon, the M72 provided the infantry with an organic bunker-busting capability.
AWM WAR/70/0596/VN.

Given their disdain for their junior ally's abilities, the Australians preferred to avoid operating with them. Moreover, if the Australians planned to manoeuvre in the vicinity of a Territorial Force unit they requested that the local government authorities confine them to their bases in order to minimise the risk of friendly fire casualties. The Australians also did not trust the provincial government's security. Consequently, in order to prevent leaks to the VC, the planners at HQ 1 ATF avoided discussing upcoming operations with South Vietnamese personnel.

The M72's rocket.
RAICM.

M72 66mm Light Anti-tank Weapon (USA)

Calibre: 66 mm
Operation:
Recoilless, shoulder fired, single shot, throw-away rocket launcher firing shaped-charge AT rocket
Length:
635 mm closed, 889 mm extended
Weight: 2.15 kg
Muzzle velocity:
144.8 m/sec
Range:
1100 m maximum range

Developed in the 1960s, the M72 was the first light weight, man-portable, shoulder-fired and discardable light anti-tank weapon. It fired a 1kg HEAT rocket that was capable of penetrating 305 mm of armour. However, in Vietnam it provided infantry with a close support weapon for use against buildings and fortifications.

Further compromising operations in Phuoc Tuy was the lack of a single chain of command and the absence of a combined staff. Instead, Australian, American and South Vietnamese commanders relied on liaison officers to coordinate their efforts against the VC. Within the province there were multiple chains of command. The Provincial Chief reported to Saigon on political concerns, but to HQ III ARVN Corps on military matters. His senior adviser was an American lieutenant-colonel who, in turn, commanded the United States advisers serving with South Vietnamese units in the province. The American advisers reported to the Civil Operations and Revolutionary Development Support organisation (CORDS) in Saigon. The Australian chain of command ran to HQ II FFV, although national command issues were the responsibility of the COMAFV. A handful of Australians served with local units as advisers in Phuoc Tuy and consequently reported to COMAFV rather than HQ 1 ATF; however almost all the advisers were American. The result was that, while the allies faced a common foe, there was never a 'total war' approach in Phuoc Tuy.

Maintenance of Aim

O. D. Jackson, now Brigadier, was 1 ATF's first commander. He identified two goals for his command:

1. to combat enemy main force units; and
2. to get among the people and provide them with the security that would lead to a better way of life.

Individually, Jackson's proposals were sound, but in combination they gave the task force two incompatible goals. Under the first goal the nature of combat was typified by conventional warfare. This goal required the Australians to undertake search and destroy missions in which they would 'find, fix, and finish' the VC—to borrow the American parlance. Jackson's second goal resembled the pacification operations conducted during the Malayan Emergency. This goal required the Australians to focus on cordon and search, interdiction, and intelligence-gathering operations. The goals represented two distinct mission types that needed different force structures, training, intellectual outlook and operational bearing. Neither Jackson nor any of his successors was able to satisfactorily resolve the inherent conflict in these objectives. Instead, they pulled the task force in different directions for the duration of its deployment. Both objectives were also manpower intensive and proved challenging for a formation that, for much of the time, had only two battalions and a base to defend.

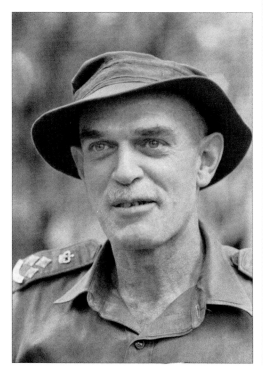

Brigadier O. D. Jackson, 1 ATF's first commander.
AWM CUN/66/0743A/VN.

To be fair, the circumstances Jackson faced in Phuoc Tuy forced him to confront the VC main forces and limited his range of actions regarding pacification. At the time of 1 ATF's arrival in Phuoc Tuy, the enemy's main force elements operated unhindered across the province. The Australians had to deal with these first if they were ever to control the countryside and protect the villages. In addition, Jackson's American superior at II FFV had no doubt that the Australians' job was to take on the enemy's main force units.

Yet according to Australian doctrine, the task force needed to win over the people in order to sever their contact with the insurgents and return their loyalty to the GVN. Jackson accepted that the main threat in Phuoc Tuy was, in actuality, not the main force units but the VC's cadre and village infrastructure. These he called the enemy's 'claws' since they were hooked into the people. The next threat level was *D445 Provincial Mobile Battalion*. He referred to this as the 'mailed fist' that backed up the village structure. The VC main forces were a danger to 1 ATF, but their destruction would not eliminate the insurgency in Phuoc Tuy.

**Brigadier S. P. Weir, COMATF September 1969 – June 1970.
AWM P01002.017.**

Also affecting 1 ATF's mission selection were the demands of its superior headquarters, namely the American II FFV. Its commander could and did assign the Australians to search and destroy missions as he saw fit. American demands did sometimes force changes to Australian plans. For example one of Brigadier S. C. Graham's objectives during his time as 1 ATF's second commander was the pacification of the Dat Do region. However, the task force also had to participate in II FFV missions such as Operation *Paddington* in the May Tao Mountains.

During the second half of his tenure, Jackson shifted his command's focus more towards pacification operations and his successor, Graham, maintained this emphasis. However, each ATF Commander had the right to determine his own operational priorities. Brigadiers R. Hughes, C. M. I Pearson, and S. P. Weir all leaned towards the destruction of the VC. Hughes, who commanded during the Tet Offensive, believed the task force's place was in the jungle while local security was the job of the South Vietnamese. According to Weir, 1 ATF's proper function was to 'get out after the regular VC and knock them out, eliminate them and separate them from the population.'

Throughout the Australians' stay in Phuoc Tuy they were under pressure to perform a multitude of tasks, often originating from different agencies. They had to shift their focus between the American priority of seeking to destroy the VC's main force units, and their own counter-insurgency philosophy of undermining the enemy's hold on the villages. The result was that operations in Phuoc Tuy were hampered by the lack of a single focus and authority for the direction of a province-wide campaign against the VC.

Mines and Booby Traps: An Ever-present Hazard

Throughout Australia's involvement in the Vietnam War mines and booby traps were among the most potent and hazardous weapons the diggers faced. The VC used mines and booby traps widely, cleverly, and offensively, and they were responsible for approximately half of all Australian casualties. For the VC, these devices offered an effective, low technology, and minimal risk method of attack that fitted comfortably within their concept of war. For the Australians, mines and booby traps were a constant concern, not only because of the casualties they caused, but also because of the stress resulting from the unpredictable nature of attack, and the psychological effect on survivors. Moreover, studies showed that the inability of diggers to strike back after losing mates to a mine or booby trap attack had a deleterious effect on unit morale.

The simplest booby trap in the VC arsenal was the Panji Trap. The trap consisted of sharpened bamboo stakes or iron spikes placed at the bottom of a hole. To improve the trap's effectiveness the VC often smeared faeces on the stakes or attached a primed grenade. The Panji Trap was a low-technology device whose components could be readily manufactured in village workshops.
Mark Wahlert.

Mines and booby traps made all movement hazardous and when these were triggered the result was often devastating. On Operation *Renmark* in the Long Hai Hills, an APC carrying men of B Company 5 RAR triggered an anti-tank mine. The force of the explosion tossed the APC into the air. It landed on its side, crushing a soldier who had been riding on top of the vehicle, its rear door blown off. As the men leapt from inside the stricken vehicle one of them stepped on an M16 anti-personnel mine which detonated, causing further casualties. It was a standard VC tactic to plant anti-personnel mines around a vehicle trap to catch anyone making a hasty exit or rushing to help the injured. The incident cost 5 RAR seven KIA and 22 WIA, including the company's commander, and the APC was destroyed.

The VC knew that local features peculiar to the region would attract foreign soldiers and encourage them to congregate and they took advantage of this tendency. During Operation *Pinnaroo* in March 1968, 5 Platoon B Company 2 RAR was investigating the ruins of a temple in the Long Hai Hills. A sapper triggered a booby trap, killing himself and wounding 13 infantrymen. The temple was a curiosity that the enemy had correctly assumed would serve as a magnet for Australian soldiers. In a single blow the VC had rendered half a platoon inoperative.

Lesson 5

There is a tendency for troops to congregate around naturally occurring or man-made points of interest, such as a ruin, watering point, market place, or choke point in a path or road. The enemy will try to exploit this attraction potential in the placement of their mines, booby traps and ambushes. The lesson is simple—avoid features of interest until declared safe, and never bunch up.

The Australians never came up with a perfect solution to mines and booby traps. In 1965, 1 RAR's commander, Brumfield, established Australia's anti-mine policy. He insisted that his men:

- go slowly and carefully;
- avoid tracks; and
- avoid the same route back.

After the establishment of the task force the Australians made two key improvements to Brumfield's initial ideas. The first was the development of specialist sapper teams known as splinter and mini-teams. Both types of teams consisted of two sappers: the splinter team went by foot while the mini-team was carried in an APC. The only difference between the two was that the vehicle-borne mini-team carried additional equipment, including mine detectors, flak jackets and helmets. Three splinter teams formed a Combat Engineer Team which the task force attached to a battalion. The splinter and mini-team concept allowed sappers to accompany infantry and APCs on patrols and thereby be immediately available for mine neutralisation.

Another easily made but deadly booby trap was the Grenade Trap. It was constructed by VC sappers who put a grenade into a can and removed the pin. The can's side held the trigger lever in place. The sapper then placed it in position, for example on top of a door frame, so that when dislodged the grenade fell from the can and exploded. The grenade could also be attached to a trip wire.
Mark Wahlert.

The VC frequently put booby traps at choke points, such as gates. When someone opened the gate the trip wire would detonate the grenade.
Mark Wahlert.

The second advancement in Australian anti-mine and booby trap policy was the greater utilisation of intelligence to counter VC mining. The VC did have preferences for where and how they laid their mines and booby traps. For example, the VC tended to avoid large defensive barriers, preferring to set mines in small clusters in an offensive manner. By studying enemy mine-laying patterns the Australians learned to avoid locations that tended to match VC laying habits.

The VC had the ability to lay mines and booby traps with remarkable speed. In one instance a column of APCs that was transporting a party of infantry crossed a stream. As they descended the bank the vehicles' bellies scraped the bank smooth. After dropping off the infantry the APCs returned to the creek and began to recross at the same point. Mid-stream the commander of the lead APC, Second Lieutenant Peter Monaghan, became suspicious. Only ten minutes had passed since the first passage but he decided to play it safe and deployed the mini-team. On the smooth bank the sappers noticed a small twig sticking up. It was the trigger for 40 pounds of high explosives. If Monaghan had proceeded, his APC would have bellied over the twig, detonated the explosives and, as there was no space between the APC and the ground, the force would have torn directly into the vehicle and probably killed everyone inside.

'Mine'. An APC carrying Australian infantry triggers a mine. Anti-tank mines were a constant danger for the task force's armoured vehicles. Huge explosive charges had the ability to flip an APC, blow off doors and hatches, and fling the crew and infantry into the air. Gouache on board.
Jeff Isaacs, OAM.

The VC never suffered from a shortage of explosives for use in booby traps. All ordnance contains a number of shells and bombs that fail to explode when discharged. While representing only a small percentage of the total, the resulting number of duds still provided the VC with an enormous reservoir of high explosives. In 1966, for example, American intelligence staff estimated that the VC recovered 27,000 tons of unexploded ordnance, much of which was available for reuse. As a consequence, in that year 1000 American servicemen died from VC booby traps.

The enemy's skilled employment of mines and booby traps affected the ability of the Australians to undertake operations. The VC went to great lengths to protect the Long Hai Hills with mines and booby traps, and units operating in this important enemy sanctuary invariably took casualties. In February 1970, during Operation *Hammersley*, 8 RAR patrols triggered two mines on the same day, resulting in 9 KIA and 12 WIA. These incidents

Lesson 7

The final lesson of mine warfare is never to assume that a route is clear, no matter how recently it has been safely traversed.

received widespread attention in Australian newspapers, became a catch-cry of the anti-war movement, were the subject of a detailed report by the COMAFV, and quickly became a political problem for the government. The result was that 1 ATF did not again challenge the VC in the Long Hai Hills.

SECURITY OPERATIONS

Securing Nui Dat

In late May 1966 elements of 1 ATF took up position at Nui Dat. The Australian base was in the heart of VC territory and sat astride the enemy's cross-province logistic network. Its security was paramount. In effect, the Australians had challenged the VC, and 1 ATF's commander, Jackson, expected the enemy to test the base's defences in the near future.

For the first two months Jackson employed 50 per cent of his infantry on patrols. Of his two battalions 5 RAR arrived first and bore the initial burden. Once 6 RAR became operational its men also shared the task. The infantry patrolled by day and night and once the monsoon started—a week after 5 RAR's arrival—through the wet.

The VC were all around Nui Dat. 5 RAR's patrols had numerous but fleeting contacts as small groups of VC were everywhere. 1 Platoon's experiences were typical. Slow, lengthy patrols would comb through scrub, jungle, or tall grass in stifling heat and humidity. Suddenly the sound of a rifle would break the silence as the forward scout spotted the enemy. The platoon would deploy immediately in sections following the contact drill they had learned in Australia, but by this time the nimble VC would have fled. The tedium did not break until the third day when 1 Platoon scored its first kill. The Australians soon modified their contact drills to include instantly applied rapid fire in the enemy's direction in the hope of catching some VC before they disappeared. If the enemy returned fire the forward observer (FO) then called in the guns.

Jackson unfolded Nui Dat's defence in three stages:

- control out to mortar range;
- control out to artillery range; and
- control of Route 2 in order to allow the safe passage of convoys between Nui Dat and Vung Tau.

Aggressive patrolling was the key element at each stage.

The houses of Long Phuoc are set on fire after the resettlement of the villagers. A 6 RAR soldier waits with his Owen Gun at the ready.
AWM CUN/66/0519/VN.

To reinforce Australian control over the countryside surrounding Nui Dat, Jackson removed the local population with the concurrence of the Province Chief. The Australians forcibly resettled the inhabitants of the two closest villages—Long Tan and Long Phuoc. Both villages were long-standing VC strongholds. Long Phuoc's guerrilla platoon offered stout resistance to the inhabitants' relocation and only succumbed after the Australians forced them from the tunnels that ran beneath the village. Jackson then declared the agricultural land surrounding the base a free fire zone in which trespassers were subject to attack without warning. These measures could not have endeared 1 ATF to the affected population and were contrary to the Australian counter-insurgency doctrine. However, by excluding the population, many of whom were in fact pro-communist, it denied the VC observation of Nui Dat and gave Australian patrols greater freedom and security in entering and exiting the base.

Probably the most difficult challenge the Australians faced in establishing Nui Dat was logistic. 1 ALSG at Vung Tau was 1 ATF's support organisation. However, 1 ALSG did not become operational until the end of April and was still in the process of establishing itself when it became responsible for 1 ATF's support. The logisticians' situation was not helped by the fact that not one unit arrived in Vietnam with a complete complement of stores, including the required 30 day reserve holding. Unit assumptions that they could demand the missing kit from the nascent 1 ALSG proved incorrect as there were no spares yet in theatre. This situation came about because units in Australia did not maintain their establishments' war-level holdings of equipment and stores. Instead, they had to requisition additional materials from the supply chain when Army Headquarters alerted them to an imminent deployment. Naturally the sudden run on stores depleted a traditionally minimally stocked supply chain, and resulted in units heading overseas without all of their equipment.

Another problem for the first inhabitants of Nui Dat was that the base was under-resourced from its inception. The Australian Army's order of battle did not contain a provision for a deployable base. The army had neither the required equipment on hand nor the personnel establishments in place to raise such a formation. In effect the task force's soldiers were double posted. The men who returned from a patrol did not receive a chance to rest but rather took their turn at building and defending the base. Additional construction engineers and an organic logistic company would have greatly eased the pressure on the combat units.

The lack of a base entitlement also complicated HQ 1 ATF's staffing levels. HQ 1 ATF received minimal—actually insufficient—staff officers to meet its many tasks, which included overseeing current and planning future operations, liaising with the GVN provincial officials and Territorial Force units and coordinating assignments and support with HQ II FFV, while at the same time maintaining the Nui Dat base. In the short term, HQ 1 ATF borrowed officers from the field units, transferring the effect of the staff shortage down the chain of command.

With only two battalions, the task force's limited numbers affected 1 ATF's operational scope. Because all units had responsibility for a section of the base's perimeter, whenever a battalion departed on an operation it left behind a defence element. The result was that platoons went on patrol not only under-strength but also under-armed, as those remaining behind required a share of the unit's heavy weapons.

Nui Dat's short-term logistic problems were solved either through the arrival of more men and materials from Australia or with the assistance of MACV. By the time of the Tet Offensive in 1968, HQ 1 ATF was able to simultaneously deploy a tactical headquarters with the two battalions operating outside of Phuoc Tuy, react to the capture of Ba Ria with its third battalion and continue to plan future operations, while also administering the base. However, these improvements took time and denied commanders the resources they needed at the start of the commitment. Most of the problems facing 1 ATF's staff, combat and logistics elements could have been avoided with better planning and forethought.

Patrolling

The cornerstone of 1 ATF's operations in Phuoc Tuy was the patrol. The Australians had no intention of sitting behind their perimeter wire waiting for the VC to come to them. Instead, Australian troops sought to control the surrounding ground, deny it to the VC and thereby exert their dominance over the enemy. Patrolling was a traditional area of Australian military excellence and the Australians used it as a means to control the battlespace. In this role it was as effective as the American reliance upon firepower—if not more so—and was certainly less expensive in lives and resources.

Aggressive patrolling had numerous benefits. It denied the enemy the element of surprise by making it difficult for them to move undetected. The Australians also used patrols to gather intelligence on the enemy, pinpoint their locations and improve the odds of success of an operation. Through their reliance on patrols the Australians were able to reach into all corners of Phuoc Tuy, including terrain which vehicles could not penetrate, and without the accompanying noise of engines to give away their presence.

Patrolling was an aspect of the art of tactics that well suited a military organisation of the nature of the Australian Army. It was a relatively inexpensive and small-scale technique that the

Australians easily adapted to their concept of war. Moreover, as a small-to-medium-size power, Australia could not afford the entire panoply of modern war—that was reserved for the great powers.

While patrolling was technically an element of tactics, the Australians extended its utility to the level of operations. Across Phuoc Tuy the task force shaped the context of the conflict using patrols to dominate the near, intermediate and distant battlefield. In addition, since Australia has always preferred to deploy a relatively small logistic footprint, the force's emphasis on patrolling allowed it to function within its support capabilities.

A variation of the patrol is the ambush. In Phuoc Tuy the ambush proved to be a highly effective and efficient means by which to attack the enemy. In fact, the rationale behind many patrols in Vietnam was to set an ambush. One COMAFV, Major-General Vincent, believed that a four to five man patrol achieved a better rate of return—in VC dead—than a battalion sweep of the countryside.

A patrol from 6 RAR/NZ (ANZAC) moves down a stream. The nearest soldier, Private Montey Paul, carries the L1A1 rifle.
AWM BEL/69/0805/VN.

In a conflict without lines, the use of patrols in combination with an ambush meant that the VC were never safe. Even senior officers were within the reach of the Australians, as evidenced on 29 April 1969 when a patrol captured *274 VC Regiment*'s executive officer.

Ambushes worked best when set by small parties in dense undergrowth along likely routes of enemy movement. The ambushers had to be heavily armed with automatic weapons, Claymore mines and trip flares in order to project a high level of fire in the few seconds available to them before the enemy took cover. Ambushes were not prolonged actions, but fast and furious strikes that relied on surprise and destroyed the enemy before they could react. Ambushes varied in size and duration. Some were overnight affairs involving only a couple of soldiers while others lasted several days and required an entire platoon. In order to avoid being ambushed themselves, the Australians followed the golden rule of never walking on tracks.

Private Brian Wruck, 2 RAR/NZ (ANZAC), sets a Claymore. Note the phrase 'front toward enemy' stamped on the mine's surface.
AWM PJE/71/0155/VN.

The llustration below depicts an ambush sprung on 21 March 1968 by 12 Platoon D Company 3 RAR during Operation *Pinnaroo*. Second Lieutenant Peatling was in command of the nine-man patrol. He positioned his M60 at the track junction to cover its multiple approaches. The bulk of the ambush party was hidden in dense vegetation parallel to one of the paths. Claymore mines added fire and depth to the perimeter. A team guarded the main body's rear, providing the small party with a 360°·defence.

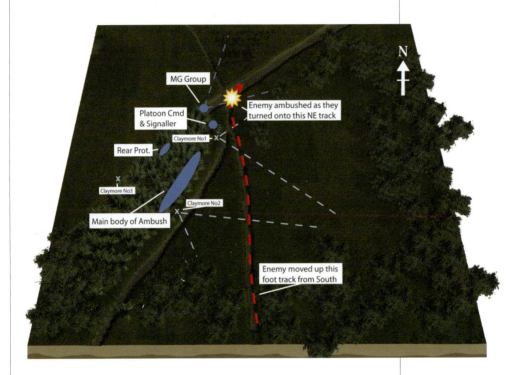

Peatling springs his ambush.
Mark Wahlert.

At 1950 hours, six VC approached the ambush position on a track from the south. The darkness was near total, and the Australians could just make out enemy silhouettes. Peatling held fire until the lead VC reached the junction and turned east onto the main track. He then detonated the Claymores and, at the same time, the M60 opened up. The next morning a sweep of the area revealed four enemy KIA, along with their weapons and equipment.

Battle of Long Tan

6 RAR began operating from Nui Dat in July 1966. Its first serious encounter with the enemy took place during Operations *Hobart I* and *II*. The objectives of the *Hobarts* were twofold. The battalion was to conduct a search and destroy sweep to the north-east of Long Tan and undertake a search and clear mission of the resettled village in order to ascertain whether there had been any VC activity amongst its ruins.

Throughout the *Hobart* operations 6 RAR made frequent contact with the enemy, and its patrols discovered numerous company-size camps. A force of VC from *D445 Provincial Mobile Battalion* bounced off C Company and, in the process of retreating, ran into B Company, which had occupied a blocking position. An intense firefight developed. The VC placed accurate 60 mm mortar fire onto the Australian position while B Company retaliated by directing artillery shells onto the enemy. The engagement lasted approximately an hour and, while B Company fought off the VC, the cost was 2 KIA and 14 WIA.

The 'Battle of Hobart' should have been an illuminative experience for 6 RAR in particular and 1 ATF in general. According to Australian counter-insurgency doctrine the enemy should have been nothing more than local bands of poorly armed and disorganised guerrillas. Instead, B Company's post-operation assessment noted:

> The VC force encountered was very quick in reacting and deployed when contact was made. Their fire and movement were good and the soldiers brave and determined. Their fire power was impressive.... Their 60 mm mortars were accurate and searched the company position thoroughly.

Instead of facing a mob, B Company had fought veteran soldiers who were willing and able to stand up to the Australians. The implication was that Vietnam was not Malaya. However, by the time of 6 RAR's next operation—Operation *Smithfield*—those involved had not yet reached that conclusion.

On 17 August Nui Dat came under 82 mm mortar and 75 mm recoilless rifle bombardment. The attack commenced at 0243 hours and lasted 22 minutes. Casualties were 22 WIA. At the time of the attack 5 RAR was in Binh Ba on Operation *Holsworthy*, and elements of 6 RAR were out on patrol. However, the VC did not follow up the bombardment with an assault.

Intelligence reports had noted increased VC activity east of Nui Dat, but the size of the enemy force and its intentions were not known. Jackson could not be sure whether the bombardment was a diversion or whether it heralded an assault on Nui Dat.

'Long Tan Action, Vietnam, 18 August 1966.' Bruce Fletcher. Oil on canvas. While the painting shows several events that happened at different points in the battle, Fletcher captures the drama of the struggle between the Australians and the VC. AWM ART40758.

Jackson's first task was to locate the enemy's firing positions and to pick up their trail. 131 Divisional Locating Battery had fixed the approximate position of the enemy's launch points; it was up to the infantry to find the exact spots.

At 0630 hours B Company 6 RAR left Nui Dat. It did not expect to be out long. The men did not carry sleeping gear and the company commander arranged a late breakfast back at the base for 0930 hours. The artillery locators had done their job well and the infantry soon found the VC's firing points. The VC, of course, were gone. Instead of returning to Nui Dat, B Company received orders to follow the enemy's tracks, a frustrating process as the VC broke up into smaller parties, doubled back, and generally took measures to throw off any pursuers.

On the following morning at about 1100 hours, D Company 6 RAR left Nui Dat with orders from the battalion commander, Lieutenant-Colonel Colin Townsend, to relieve B Company and take over the search. At 1300 hours the two companies joined. After a briefing between the two commanders over lunch, B Company headed back to Nui Dat. D Company's commander, Major Harry Smith, decided to follow enemy tracks to the north-east towards the Long Tan rubber plantation.

At 1500 hours D Company entered the plantation, moving carefully through the rubber trees with 11 Platoon leading. First contact occurred at 1540 hours when a VC patrol walked into 11 Platoon's perimeter. The Australians opened fire and the VC fled east. After a pause to reorganise from patrol to pursuit formation, 11 Platoon followed. The diggers had not gone far when they came under heavy fire and went to ground, immediately establishing an all-round defence. The platoon commander, Lieutenant Gordon Sharpe, reported to company headquarters that he was engaged by an enemy force of approximately platoon size. As the incoming fire increased and was augmented by machine-gun and mortar fire, and with the enemy working around their position, it became obvious that this was an underestimate. D Company's FO, the New Zealander Major Morrie Stanley, alerted the guns at Nui Dat and began to bring shells down around 11 Platoon.

11 Platoon was in trouble. In the haste of the pursuit it had moved beyond the support range of the rest of the company. Enemy insurgents ringed its position; fire poured in from front and flanks; the monsoon opened up and heavy rain reduced visibility to mere metres; Sharpe lay dead, shot through the head, and command had passed to Sergeant Bob Buick; more than a third of the platoon were casualties. The Australians had begun the encounter under the assumption that they were the aggressors. Instead they now fought for survival against the entire *275 VC Regiment*.

Smith sent forward 10 Platoon to help extract 11 Platoon, but it in turn ran into an enemy flanking party which forced it back to its start point. Smith then tried the other flank. 12 Platoon first jigged south and then headed east towards 10 Platoon's position. It too ran into a large enemy force which had manoeuvred behind 11 Platoon. 12 Platoon took cover, itself nearly surrounded.

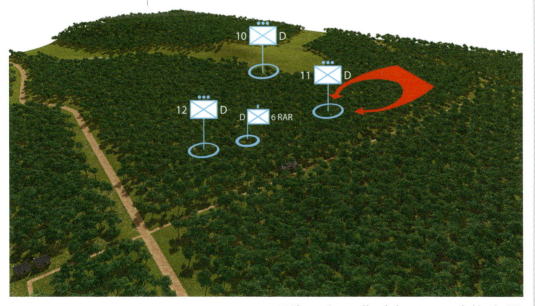

11 Platoon is cut off and almost surrounded by the VC.
Mark Wahlert.

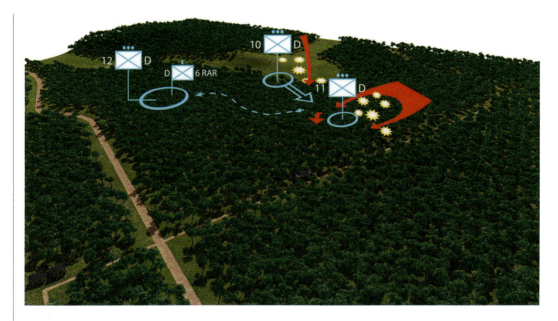

10 Platoon is bounced by the VC as it moves to 11 Platoon's aid.
Mark Wahlert.

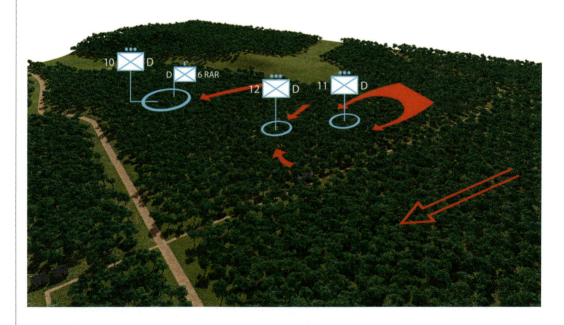

12 Platoon fails to reach 11 Platoon and fights for its own life. Other VC
manoeuvre to surround D Company HQ.
Mark Wahlert.

Buick steadfastly maintained his position, keeping the enemy at bay with platoon fire and massive support from an entire field regiment of guns firing from Nui Dat. No one had panicked. Some men had run out of ammunition and lay in the mud with a machete or grenade waiting for the enemy to close. At 1730 Buick decided to risk the enemy's fire and fall back. It was not a textbook manoeuvre, but a race by those who could still run out of the killing zone and towards the rest of the company. 11 Platoon fortuitously found 12 Platoon, and the two groups together fell back on the company headquarters.

With his company concentrated, Smith awaited the enemy's assault. His soldiers manned a 360° defence, and by now everyone knew that they were heavily outnumbered. D Company's extinction was imminent. However, just as another column of VC prepared to rush forward, the diggers heard the noise of approaching engines. The APCs of 3 Troop, carrying A Company 6 RAR, burst onto the scene. Surprised by the armoured vehicles' appearance, and with Australian 50 calibre machine-guns cutting through their ranks, the VC broke heart and fled into the evening's advancing gloom. In fact, this was the second enemy force that 3 Troop had intercepted. A little earlier the APCs had driven through *D445 Provincial Mobile Battalion* and scattered the VC as they manoeuvred to envelop D Company.

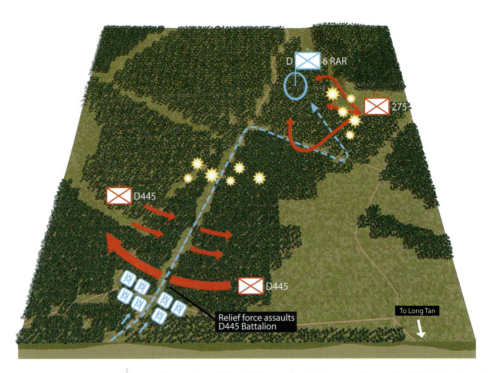

The arrival of the APCs carrying A Company forces the VC to break contact. The timely arrival of reinforcements saves D Company. Mark Wahlert.

The APCs' arrival saved D Company. The VC were massing for an assault that would have most likely destroyed the entire company. Instead of annihilation, however, D Company savoured an outstanding victory over a far more numerous opponent.

There were a number of key reasons for the Australian success:

1. Arguably the most important pieces of equipment D Company carried as it left Nui Dat were the AN/PRC 25 radio sets borne by the unit's signallers. With them the company FO brought to bear the power of a field regiment. Communications were also essential in providing D Company the ability to report its situation to headquarters, and in 1 ATF's coordination of its relief.

2. The gunners of 1 Field Regiment worked heroically and tirelessly throughout the engagement and provided D Company with the firepower it needed to survive. Time after time, well-directed shells tore apart the enemy ranks and broke up their concentrations.

3. In the dark, in the midst of a torrential monsoonal downpour and in the face of VC ground fire, two RAAF helicopter crews braved atrocious flying conditions and airdropped critically needed ammunition to D Company. Had these helicopters not made the flight the infantry would most likely have run out of ammunition before the APCs reached them.

4. The timely arrival of the APCs saved D Company from a mass assault. The arrival of these powerful vehicles broke the enemy's will to continue the fight. Long Tan confirmed the importance of armour in Vietnam and demonstrated the need to possess a fast-moving, hard-hitting resource.

5. Upon contact, the infantry immediately adopted an all-round defence. In a conflict which lacked fixed lines, units had to protect their own flanks and rear against an enemy that could strike from any direction.

6. D Company's application of firepower allowed its men to inflict horrific casualties on the enemy. The diggers stood firm and repeatedly broke up enemy attacks with their weapons. The next morning the Australians counted nearly 250 VC dead and gathered large piles of enemy weapons and equipment. The Australian casualties amounted to 18 KIA and 24 WIA.

The Battle of Long Tan illustrated the power of modern weapons, the importance of sound small-unit tactics, and the magnification of their effect when used in combination. In addition, the Australian infantry did not bend, no member of D Company attempted to slip away into the dark, every soldier stood firm and fulfilled his role. These attributes were a testament to the force's high morale and to the men's training.

However, the course of the encounter revealed some faults in 1 ATF preparation and its response to the battle. When combat began, there was no ready reaction force at Nui Dat. Instead, A Company, which had just returned from a three-day patrol, received hasty orders to get back out, borne by the APCs which themselves had also been given sudden orders. After Long Tan, 1 ATF instituted a policy of having a pre-designated company, with armour support, standing by either to respond to a VC attack, or to strike at an enemy target of opportunity.

During the battle there was a delay in the RAAF helicopters' departure because no one at HQ 1 ATF had anticipated the requirement for an air-portable prepacked resupply. Instead, 6 RAR personnel had to pull and pack stores on the run. After the battle 1 ATF corrected this omission.

Troops of 6 RAR examine some of the weapons abandoned by the VC after the Battle of Long Tan. The weapons include a heavy MG, several RPG launchers and numerous rifles.
AWM FOR/66/0667/VN.

During the battle the VC employed 60 mm mortars to bombard the Australian positions. Since mortars were no longer part of an Australian company's establishment the VC had a significant advantage. An Australian battalion did contain 81 mm mortars, but they belonged to the support company. In the post-battle assessment, consideration was given to issuing 60 mm mortars to rifle companies. Mortars would provide a rifle company with the ability to bring bombs down on an enemy which had closed within the safety margin of the artillery. This step was rightly rejected because a mortar's weight and ammunition requirements would have compromised a company's patrolling abilities. Instead, the infantrymen received the American M79 grenade launcher.

After the battle 1 ATF continued Operation *Smithfield*, hoping to catch the remnants of *275 VC Regiment* and *D445 Provincial Mobile Battalion* before they reached their sanctuaries. However, the enemy had escaped.

Privates Colin Dennison and Max Drain ready their APC-borne 81 mm mortar for firing.
AWM CRO/68/0250/VN.

Mortar, M29 81mm Mortar (USA & North Vietnam)

Calibre: 81 mm
Operation:
  Muzzle loaded, drop fired, smooth-bore
Crew: 3
Weight:
  Barrel 12.7 kg, bipod 18.14 kg, baseplate 11.8 kg
Rate of fire:
  Up to 8-10 rpm
Range: 3625 m (HE)

The US M29 mortar was adopted by the Australian Army in the early 1960s. In Vietnam it was employed by the mortar platoon of each battalion. It fired a wide range of ammunition types inluding: high explosive, fragmentation, white phosphorus, and smoke. As well as being fired from the ground the M29 could also be mounted in and fired from the M125A1 Mortar Carrier.

The high level of fatalities the Australians had inflicted on the VC had not gone unnoticed by the Americans. To inflict further destruction on a beaten opponent HQ II FFV organised a search and destroy operation. Operation *Toledo* commenced on 23 August and lasted until 8 September. Joining 1 ATF was 173 Airborne Brigade (Separate), elements of 1 Infantry Division (US), 1/26 USMC, and two ARVN ranger battalions. The Australians found nothing, although the evidence of the American presence was overwhelming. The 5 RAR battalion historian commented:

> helicopters buzzed to and fro, light spotting aircraft cruised constantly overhead, and occasionally larger aircraft ... packed with radio locating, infra red and photographic equipment moved ... across the sky ... it must have been fairly obvious to the Viet Cong that they were being sought by a force of such size that they would have been wise to avoid us.

Long Tan was a comprehensive Australian victory. The Australians inflicted heavy casualties on the enemy, and, more importantly, taught the VC a bloody lesson. When 6 RAR ran into the VC in the plantation they interrupted an enemy build-up the objective of which was the annihilation of the Australian base. The victory not only pre-empted this offensive, but the magnitude of the Australian success meant that the VC never again planned a serious challenge to Nui Dat.

6 RAR soldiers supported by an APC attempt to locate the VC after the Battle of Long Tan in Operation *Smithfield*.
AWM CUN/66/0706/VN.

FSBs and The Horseshoe

Fire support bases (FSBs) were a regular feature of Australian operations. In a war with no fixed lines and an elusive enemy, the Australians had to operate away from Nui Dat in order to reach the VC. However it would have been both dangerous and foolish for them to move beyond the range of their artillery. When Jackson established Nui Dat he instigated the policy that the infantry would not patrol outside the reach of the base's mortars and guns.

Yet Jackson did not intend for the task force to remain behind the wire of Nui Dat, waiting for their guns to destroy any VC that approached. His orders were to control Phuoc Tuy. To accomplish this, the Australians had to operate anywhere in the province, even within the enemy's strongholds where unsupported infantry would have been a tempting target for the VC. Therefore, if the task force were to secure its TAOR it was necessary for it to extend the range of its guns.

Five M2A2 howitzers engage a target from FSB Pamela. Note the FSB's temporary earthen walls.
AWM PJE/71/0317/VN.

The establishment of temporary FSBs allowed 1 ATF to exploit two of its advantages over the VC—firepower and manoeuvrability—and in so doing allowed the guns to reach any point the task force desired. Usually when an operation took place beyond the range of the guns at Nui Dat or The Horseshoe, at least one battery deployed to a temporary FSB within support range of the mission's area of operations (AO). The Australians quickly effected the movement either by vehicle tow or American heavy lift helicopter. Once the FSB was active, helicopters provided for its resupply. A new FSB's location could not be kept hidden from the VC so aerial resupply was not a liability. A FSB, therefore, was a mobile artillery platform that moved across Phuoc Tuy according to operational requirement.

A FSB also needed protection, however. At its most basic a FSB was a battery of guns protected by an infantry covering party, usually drawn from the battalion that the artillery was supporting. While the infantry guarded the FSB, the gunners, in turn, stood ready to fire in support of friendly forces patrolling within the AO. The Australians also employed more elaborate FSBs depending on the operational situation. For example, during the Tet Offensive, FSB Coral contained a battalion of infantry, a field regiment of guns, along with engineer, APC and tank elements.

The Horseshoe.
AWM P01353.040.

While most FSBs were temporary, there was one exception—The Horseshoe. This FSB contained a 105 mm artillery battery protected by an infantry company. Its construction commenced in March 1967 as a preliminary step in the building of the minefield barrier. The FSB sat on top of the remnant volcanic crater on the northern outskirts of Dat Do. Although only 60 metres high, it towered over the surrounding paddy fields, and from its top the Australians enjoyed a 360° view out to a distance of about five kilometres. It was highly defensible and attacking VC would have had to advance up a gradient that averaged two in one. The Horseshoe was also within range of Nui Dat and the two bases were able to mutually support each other.

After the mine barrier's failure, 1 ATF continued to occupy The Horseshoe. Dat Do was the epicentre of considerable VC activity, and nearby features such as a stretch of jungle known as the 'Long Green' and the Long Hai Hills contained enemy installations. The Dat Do region was a regular AO for the task force and the diggers relied on The Horseshoe's guns for support.

The Horseshoe's liabilities were its isolation and the fact that it exacerbated the workload of 1 ATF's already overstretched infantry. The first problem was in part offset through the regular rotation of its garrison. However, for the second there was no easy answer, and the infantry had to accept another call on their labour. The Australians occupied The Horseshoe until its handover to the ARVN in June 1971.

Route Security: Operation *Robin*

The protection of Route 15 was one of the core responsibilities given to the task force in the operation agreement negotiated between the Australians and MACV. The highway was an important link in American communications, joining the harbour of Vung Tau to the Saigon–Bien Hoa area. As the United States commitment expanded, the congestion at Saigon's riverside quays became a growing concern for HQ MACV. To ease the backlog the Americans decided to use Vung Tau as a secondary port. Once ashore, newly arrived units transited to their AOs via Route 15 across Phuoc Tuy. If the Americans were to continue their build-up unhindered, the Australians had to keep the road secure.

The most vulnerable point in Phuoc Tuy for convoys occurred when they passed through the narrow coastal corridor between the mangrove swamps of the Rung Sat and the jungle-clad hills of the Nui Dinh, Nui Thi Vai and Nui Ong Trinh formations. Both sides of the road provided close cover in which a VC ambush or rocket-propelled grenade (RPG) party could hide, or protection for sappers to creep forward in the night to plant mines and booby traps. In addition, from the nearby high ground the VC had a clear line of sight over much of the road, giving them an early warning of convoy movements. The hills also provided many potential mortar positions.

Between 11 and 16 October 1966, 1 ATF undertook a road security task known as Operation *Robin*. The task force's job was to secure Route 15 for the passage of 3 Brigade 4 Infantry Division (US). The task force units involved were:

- 5 RAR
- 6 RAR (A & D companies)
- 2 Troop 1 APC Squadron
- 103 Field Battery
- Battery A 2/35 Artillery (US)
- 1 Field Squadron (elements)
- one H13 161 (Indep) Recce Flight
- six UH-1Bs 9 Squadron RAAF.

As a preliminary to Operation *Robin*, 5 RAR conducted Operation *Canberra* over the period 6 to 10 October. This was a search and destroy mission in the Nui Thi Vai and Nui Ong Trinh Hills which overlooked the road. 5 RAR's objective was to clear the VC from the heights so that they could not observe 3 Brigade's transit, nor use the heights as a base for a mortar or rocket attack. The diggers fought a pitched battled with a VC platoon and destroyed base camps capable of holding a battalion. The Australian losses were 13 WIA.

Operation *Robin* followed immediately after *Canberra*. The Australians' AO ran along Route 15 from Ba Ria to the village of Phu My, a distance of approximately 20 kilometres. After Phu My, the road's security became the responsibility of 173 Airborne Brigade (Separate). Intelligence reports estimated that the probable enemy strength in the area was the local force *Chau Duc District Company*. It was believed that the nearest VC main force unit was at least 10 kilometres away.

5 RAR divided its AO into five sub-areas. Battalion headquarters, the mortar platoon and attached guns remained at a FSB outside the village of Ap Ong Trinh, approximately the mid-point of the AO. This had been their position during Operation *Canberra*. The battalion's anti-tank and pioneer platoons provided soldiers for the FSB's defence. Each of 5 RAR's companies received a sub-area of its own. Under command of each company was an APC section and a detachment of engineers. Providing the task force's coverage from Ap Phu Hai to Ba Ria was A Company 6 RAR with its own APC and engineer support. D Company

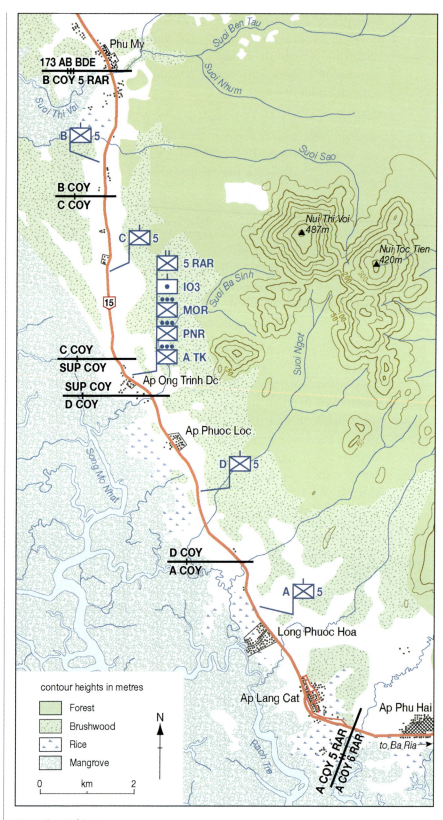

Operation *Robin*.
Kay Dancey.

6 RAR's task was to provide distant patrol of the Nui Dinh Hill area. Its mission was to prevent VC from observing the road or using the high ground as a fire base. It would also provide warning if a large VC force moved into the area. Moving through the jungle-clad foothill zone were patrols from 3 SAS Squadron whose task was to set ambushes and provide early warning of the enemy's approach. Lastly, serving as the rapid reaction force at Nui Dat was a third 6 RAR company. Operation *Robin*, therefore, involved nearly the entire task force, except for those elements required for the defence of Nui Dat.

On 10 October the Australians moved into their AOs by vehicle and helicopter insertion. Commencing on 11 October, the Americans started pushing two convoys a day over the route. Each day followed a similar pattern. In the morning the Australians moved out of their company leaguers and secured the road. The Australians searched for booby traps that might have been laid in the night or disturbances that would signal the infiltration of a VC ambush party. Further out in the jungle and the hills the SAS and 6 RAR set ambushes or watched for signs of enemy activity.

Each company commander had at his call considerable fire assets. Under direct command was the attached section of APCs. Next up the firepower chain was 5 RAR's mortars and its supporting artillery batteries. From their FSB the gunners reached all points in the AO. In addition, the Americans made available a team of light fire helicopters. The Australians employed the gunships on four occasions, using them to neutralise suspected VC positions. In case of a night-time contact the Australians also had access to a firefly—an illumination helicopter. Lastly, the Australians could call on bomber and other air support as needed. On 11 October 5 RAR called in two air strikes on suspected VC positions.

The Americans varied the departure time of their convoys in order to avoid establishing a pattern that the VC could anticipate. Enemy resistance proved light and 3 Brigade crossed Phuoc Tuy unmolested. The Australians did encounter some VC, but mostly at a distance, and no contact developed into a serious action. It was helicopters and H13 aircraft that received most of the enemy's attention. Several aircraft were hit by ground fire with one H13 shot down, injuring the pilot and his passenger. The main danger to the Australians lay in the mines and booby traps that infested the road, culverts and surrounding ground.

Lesson 9

In route security operations it is critical to control not only the road but also the surrounding terrain. Security forces must dominate the ground out to the effective range of the enemy's weapons if a convoy is to pass without risk.

Even without a significant enemy challenge, Operation *Robin* was a major undertaking for the task force. In order to be effective, road security operations require the allocation of tremendous resources. They are both manpower and machine intensive because of the necessity to control not just the road's immediate perimeter but also the entire battlespace out to the effective range of the enemy's weapons. Even though it faced at most a single company of local VC, the mission consumed nearly all of the task force's available strength. The enemy's task was far easier. The VC could pick the point at which to strike and required far fewer resources to accomplish their mission.

Operation *Robin* was a success because the Australians dedicated the resources they needed to conduct close, intermediate and distant patrolling which kept the VC away. The enemy could have challenged the convoy's passage, but the Australians had made the effort too difficult and risky for them to attempt. Quickly following on Operation *Robin* were two more road security operations (*Canary* and *Duck*). For each, the Australians followed the pattern laid down during *Robin*. The results were the same: the safe transit of Route 15 by American reinforcements.

TARGETING VC LOGISTICS

VC Logistics

As light infantry, the VC did not require the massive support that the firepower-intensive and mobility-dependent American and, to a lesser extent, Australian forces did. Yet, while comparatively lightly armed, the VC soldier's effectiveness still depended on the operation of an efficient logistic organisation. To conduct the war, therefore, the VC created and maintained a support network that sourced required materials from the international, national, and local markets and distributed them to units across the war zone.

The most concrete link in the VC logistic system was the Ho Chi Minh Trail. The Trail began in North Vietnam, ran for most of its length through Laos and Cambodia, and terminated in the delta region of the south.

North Vietnam began construction of the Ho Chi Minh Trail in 1959. In 1965, with the American build-up, the North began to expand the Trail's capacity. Thousands of labourers transformed what had been a track that took six months to walk from end to end into a highway capable of supporting thousands of trucks with a transit time of one week. Southwards over this route came tens of thousands of North Vietnamese soldiers and modern war materials provided to the communists by their Soviet and Chinese allies.

'Digger on Patrol, 7 RAR, Operation *Forrest*', Ken McFadyen. Charcoal on paper. The drawing shows a digger setting out on a patrol during Operation *Forrest*. The artist draws attention to the soldier's four water bottles, a typical load.
AWM ART40658.

The United States Air Force undertook a massive bombing campaign against the Ho Chi Minh Trail, flying into the face of an integrated air defence system. It failed, however, to halt the transit of men and supplies. Air power could not permanently cut the route, nor inflict casualties and damage greater than the level the North Vietnamese were willing to accept. Strategically, the air offensive was a failure.

While the Ho Chi Minh Trail was a key element of the communist logistic infrastructure, it was not the sole source of supplies for VC units fighting in South Vietnam. Insurgency movements are built on the support of the local people. It is the village that provides much of the manpower, materials and especially food that an insurgent soldier needs to survive. Giap and other communist leaders in Hanoi understood that their war effort depended on the village for the insurgency's human and material resources. Australian doctrine recognised this local dynamic and remained underpinned by the tenet that an insurgency's access to local political, logistic, manpower and intelligence assets was a prerequisite for the movement's success.

In accordance with communist insurgency theory, the VC created an extensive support base in Phuoc Tuy. They established installations including bomb factories to convert explosives removed from duds into booby traps and mines, weapon repair facilities, hospitals, rest centres, and all manner of storage depots and distribution points. Many were underground, either hidden in natural features such as the caves of the Long Hai Hills, or in purpose-built tunnels dug beneath hidden camps. In addition, the province's villages contained various committees that provided material support to the insurgents in the field and served as a source for new recruits.

To acquire the necessary materials the VC maintained a system of tax collectors, purchase agents, suppliers and intelligence officers who worked under the direction of village, district, and provincial committees. To distribute these materials the VC also maintained a network of trails that linked depots with field units.

The Minefield Barrier

1 ATF could do nothing about the Ho Chi Minh Trail. Even had the Australians possessed the assets to attack the Trail, most of its route was off-limits in Laos and Cambodia. However, the disruption of the VC's local and regional support network lay within 1 ATF's purview. Virtually all Australian operations had some logistic objective: the seizure of weapons and rice, for example, or the

destruction of enemy installations. The Australians used these attacks to reduce the enemy's ability to operate in and around Phuoc Tuy, thereby contributing to the province's security.

One of the largest, and also most controversial, anti-VC logistic actions undertaken by 1 ATF was the construction of the minefield barrier. Running between the villages of Dat Do and Lang Phuoc Hai, its construction was the work of the task force's second commander, Graham.

Brigadier Stuart Graham, 1 ATF's second commander.
AWM EKT/67/0041/VN.

Graham was a firm adherent to Australian counter-insurgency doctrine. Jackson had successfully established the task force in the heart of Phuoc Tuy and pushed VC main force units to the province's periphery. Graham decided that the next step was to maintain and broaden the separation between the communist field units and the people. He believed that this would lead inexorably to the reduction of the enemy's units, the breaking down of the VC village organisation, and the strengthening of ties between the people and the GVN.

In planning his operations Graham sought to reduce the emphasis on search and destroy operations. He accepted that any attempt to bring the VC to battle was unlikely to be productive because:

- he did not know the VC's location; and
- if he did locate the VC, the enemy usually avoided contact by slipping away into the jungle.

Instead of attacking the VC directly, Graham decided to interdict the link between the enemy's field units and the province's villages. He believed that this would leave the VC with only two options. Either they had to break the Australian interdiction of their supplies by offering battle, and thereby expose themselves to Australian firepower, or suffer a gradual decline leading to their destruction from lack of support.

The most important source of supplies for the VC in Phuoc Tuy was the area around Dat Do, which was the province's granary. Dat Do, and other nearby villages, contained extensive VC organisations, numerous sympathisers, and well-armed guerrillas. Across the zone, VC loyalists collected, stored and carried supplies to main force units via a network of foot and ox cart trails. In addition, the sector provided easy access to the VC bases in the Long Hai Hills.

With only two battalions under command, Graham did not have sufficient infantry to prevent enemy movements in the Dat Do region by patrolling. Instead, he decided to employ a static barrier as a substitute for manpower. When completed, the fence began at the edge of The Horseshoe feature, swung around the eastern side of Dat Do, ran south, passing near the villages Phuoc Loi and Hoi My, and ended near the sea with the fishing settlement of Lang Phuoc Hai. Along its course it intercepted routes 23, 44 and 326. The only gap in the fence was a swampy sector between the villages of Phuoc Loi and Hoi My where the ground provided a natural barrier to movement.

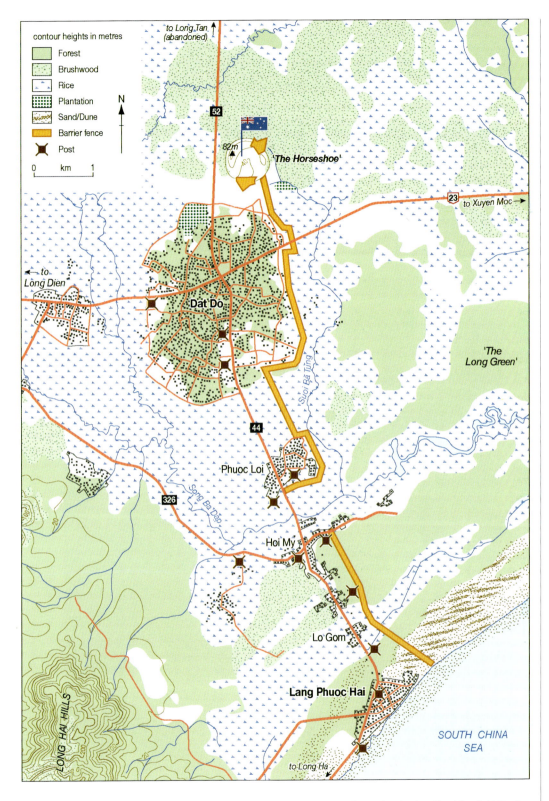

contour heights in metres

Forest
Brushwood
Rice
Plantation
Sand/Dune
Barrier fence
Post

N

0   km   1

to Long Tan
(abandoned)

52

82 m

'The Horseshoe'

23   to Xuyen Moc →

to
Long Dien →

Dat Do

Suoi Ba Tung

'The
Long Green'

44

Phuoc Loi

Song Ba Dap

326

Hoi My

Lo Gom

LONG HAI HILLS

Lang Phuoc Hai

SOUTH CHINA
SEA

to Long Ha

Operation *Leeton*: The Minefield Barrier.
Kay Dancey.

The code name for the project was Operation *Leeton*. It commenced on 6 March 1967 and ended on 1 June 1967, and its first stage was the establishment of The Horseshoe FSB. Artillery fire from The Horseshoe covered the troops constructing the fence.

The barrier consisted of two parallel double rows of wire in which the Australians piled bundles of concertina to a height of around two metres. Approximately 75 metres of open ground separated the two corridors. In the intervening ground, except where it was too wet, the Australians planted over 20,000 M16A1 anti-personnel mines. Laid with many of the mines was an M26 grenade as part of an anti-lifting device. 1 Field Squadron undertook the minefield's construction.

M16A1 Anti-Personnel Land Mine (USA)

Operation:
    Hand laid fragmentation bounding land mine
Weight: 3.83 kg
Height:
    190 mm (with M605 fuse fitted)
Diameter: 100 mm
Casualty radius: 30 m
Danger area: 200 m

The M16A1 land mine entered Australian service in 1967 with the laying of the Minefield Barrier. It requires 3.6 to 9 kg of pressure to detonate. The mine then flies upwards and explodes at approximately one metre above ground level.

Two assault pioneers, Corporal Trent Grall (l) and Lance Corporal Barry O'Brien (r) of 7 RAR, prime M16A1 mines for the Minefield Barrier.
AWM P01783.003.

To help protect the barrier the Australians built additional platoon and company-sized fortified posts for the local Regional and Popular Forces. The fence had only three crossing points, each adjacent to a Territorial Force post whose task was to inspect passing traffic. The plan was for the fence to channel traffic to inspection points, thereby preventing the VC from moving supplies out of the Dat Do region.

For the first six months after its completion the minefield barrier caused a dramatic decline in VC traffic. Intelligence reports estimated that it had reduced enemy supply movements by approximately 80 per cent. The VC, on the other hand, recognised the danger and could not let Graham's creation go unchallenged. However, instead of offering the Australians battle, the VC countered the barrier's effectiveness with a third option. They cut gaps in the fence, opened safe passageways through the minefield, and restored the flow of supplies.

The VC's reaction exploited the great flaw in Graham's scheme. The task force might have constructed the fence, but upon its completion its primary defence and maintenance passed to GVN provincial authorities. This responsibility in turn devolved onto the shoulders of the small ARVN battalion that garrisoned Dat Do, and nearby Regional and Popular Force companies and platoons.

The assignment of the fence's protection to this particular ARVN battalion was unfortunate. This was an extremely low quality unit whose employment in garrison duty signalled its unfitness for field work. The battalion did not patrol effectively—when it patrolled at all—and it certainly never did so to Australian standards. Compounding this problem was the preference of the Regional Force and Popular Force units to remain inside the protection of their posts. 1 ATF knew of the ARVN's failure to patrol the fence, yet the Australian infantry company on The Horseshoe did not itself attempt to protect the barrier. Thus the Australians, content to leave the task to South Vietnamese Forces, did not compensate for their ally's known inadequacies.

Assisting the VC was the failure of the anti-lifting devices to function properly, as the moist soil deactivated the M26 grenade. In effect, the minefield became an ordnance depot for the VC who replanted the mines that they removed elsewhere, often with tragic addition to the Australian casualty toll. The environs of Dat Do became particularly hazardous, and Australian casualties in this area increased markedly after the minefield's subversion.

The VC worked swiftly. By the beginning of 1968, 1 ATF staff admitted that the barrier was ineffective. In 1969 it became a political problem for the government, and was the subject of heated debate in Parliament.

Graham's idea for the barrier fence was a good one. It conformed to the Australian concept of counter-insurgency warfare and struck at an enemy point of vulnerability. Moreover, it was a low casualty risk operation that promised to reap benefits far greater than its costs. The VC's quick reaction to its construction suggested that the scheme had rightly targeted one of the enemy's sensitive points.

However, the barrier scheme suffered from design and implementation problems that doomed it to failure. Once constructed it was unclear whether the barrier was simply an obstacle to movement or a minefield protected by a fence. In fact, it must be questioned whether the mines were necessary at all. All Graham wanted was a barrier to movement that forced traffic to choke points for inspection. This could have been accomplished without the mines, or perhaps with only a limited number of booby traps placed in the wire. Moreover, a properly patrolled wire barrier would have survived equally as well as one backed up by mines and would have posed less risk to the Australians.

The second problem was that while the Provincial authorities accepted responsibility for the barrier's protection, they never had a stake in the project. The South Vietnamese did not conceive or build it and, therefore, never owned it. In addition, from the perspective of Vietnamese culture and the need to maintain good alliance relations, the provincial authorities did not have the option of refusing to take on responsibility for the barrier's defence, no matter the deficiencies of their forces. The Australians held the capabilities of their junior partner in disdain and were aware of their weaknesses in patrolling. However, this did not stop Graham from handing to his ally a task for which it was not suited. Graham had come up with a promising idea, one that was worth trying, but he had failed to think through the plan to its logical conclusion.

Lesson 10

Ownership matters. An ally is more likely to take responsibility for an asset or task if they have a stake in its creation and maintenance. Moreover, once operational control is handed over to a junior ally or even a contractor, it is essential to monitor the situation to ascertain that the job is being done to your own standard.

Operation *Forrest*

In mid-1967 American intelligence officers concluded that rice denial was an effective method by which to curtail VC operations. In late 1967, during Operations *Kenmore* and *Santa Fe*, 1 ATF gained intelligence that pointed to the VC's intention to increase rice procurement activities. As a result of these developments, the then 1 ATF Commander, Brigadier Hughes, decided to prevent the VC from gathering the harvest.

Brigadier Ron Hughes, COMATF, at the village of Phu My during Operation *Forrest*. He is speaking with the CO of 7 RAR, Lieutenant-Colonel Eric Smith. AWM THU/67/1238/VN.

Rice formed the basis of the Vietnamese diet and its possession was a necessity for the success of the VC war effort. Hughes believed that if 1 ATF controlled the rice harvest it would have a flow-on effect on the enemy's capacity to operate in Phuoc Tuy. At a minimum, success would force enemy insurgents to spend more of their time on food acquisition tasks rather than insurgency actions. In addition, increased food taxation demands on farmers might help turn the populace against the VC.

Operation *Forrest* was Australia's first rice denial effort since 1 RAR's Operation *New Life* in 1965. It ran from 23 November 1967 to 5 January 1968, the peak of the harvest, and employed both of 1 ATF's battalions. Hughes divided the province in two halves along the Route 2 axis. He tasked 2 RAR with the east zone and 7 RAR with the west.

The operation divided into a number of sub-operations, mostly cordon and search of villages and the patrol and ambush of likely enemy staging areas and approach routes. On 24 November, for example, 7 RAR searched Hoa Long. The village was known to contain a VC infrastructure, and the battalion detained nine suspects. In Hoa Long one of the battalion's tasks was to ascertain whether villagers were storing excessive quantities of rice; any surplus to need might be destined for VC consumption. Shifting rapidly across the province the battalions also searched the villages of Phu My, Ong Trinh, and Phuoc Hoa, amongst others.

It is difficult to ascertain whether Operation *Forrest* had a lasting effect on VC operations in 1 ATF's TAOR. While it resulted in the identification of numerous VC sympathisers and the seizure of weapons and equipment, its effect on the larger strategic picture is less clear. Within two months of the operation's conclusion the VC launched the Tet Offensive. Phuoc Tuy's role in these attacks was relatively minor, probably not because of a local shortage of rice but due to the fact that Tet's centre of gravity lay elsewhere. Yet, while the VC in Phuoc Tuy were not as active during Tet as they were elsewhere, they still attacked the provincial capital of Ba Ria and were defeated only after bitter urban fighting.

Throughout Operation *Forrest*, with one exception, there were only minor and fleeting contacts with the enemy. The exception occurred on 27 November when D Company 7 RAR fought a pitched battle with the *Chau Duc District Company*. The encounter followed the SAS's discovery of an enemy-occupied camp about 12 kilometres south-west of Nui Dat. The SAS assessment was that the camp held between 15 and 20 logistic personnel. 7 RAR was tasked with eliminating the outpost. In support was 106 Battery which deployed to FSB Alpha in order to be within range.

On the morning of 27 November helicopters lifted B and D Companies to their insertion point. To avoid arousing the enemy's suspicion, the infantry landed some distance from the target, and had an eight-hour approach march through incessant rain. While the rain was uncomfortable it did provide a tactical benefit. It helped cover the Australians' approach and lulled enemy sentries into a false sense of security. As one digger pointed out, 'Who else walked all day in the steaming rain?'

> Lesson 11
>
> The ability to operate in adverse conditions is an advantage that a combatant can exploit against a less hardy opponent. Commanders should instil among their soldiers an acceptance that discomfort is preferable to becoming a casualty. Effective leaders will never miss an opportunity to gain an edge over the enemy, even if it entails additional hardship.

By 1700 hours the Australians were at their start line. The plan called for D Company, with 10 and 12 Platoons leading, to assault the camp and dislodge the VC. B Company was given the main killing responsibility. It set ambushes on probable escape routes, planning to hit the enemy as they fled. From experience the Australians knew that small bodies of VC invariably ran when attacked. In order to preserve surprise, 106 Battery did not fire a preliminary bombardment.

As soon as D Company made contact, however, the plan unravelled. The defenders did not break as predicted. Instead they mounted a stout defence, pouring fire onto the Australians from their bunkers and connecting trenches. D Company took casualties but fought its way into the centre of the enemy's position. 12 Platoon cleared one bunker with an M72, killing two VCs, and assaulted a second using fire and movement. At one point 12 Platoon was unable to manoeuvre because of the volume of enemy fire and had to be assisted by 10 Platoon. But the Australians gradually gained the upper hand and the surviving VC broke contact. D Company now listened for the sound of B Company springing the trap.

Unexpectedly, however, the enemy continued to fail to behave according to the Australian plan. Instead of fleeing to their destruction at the hands of B Company, the VC looped back around the camp and counter-attacked 10 and 12 Platoons from the flank and rear. The platoons had been slow to establish an all-round defence and neglected to utilise the camp's bunkers and trenches as strong points. In addition, 11 Platoon had not closed up and the VC exploited this gap in the Australian position.

The VC attack was violent: RPG rounds detonated in trees, causing shrapnel to rain down on the Australians while automatic rifle fire swept the ground. Casualties mounted quickly and it was in this second phase that both Australian fatalities occurred. The platoons were not helped by having three of their M60s out of action from faults, despite the desperate action of the gunners to repair the weapons. The enemy's barrage ceased only when they exhausted their ammunition and withdrew. Only one of B Company's ambushes was successful, killing two female VC.

Lesson 12

The enemy is not required to act according to the role assigned to them in the plan. Commanders must remember that no plan survives initial contact with the enemy.

The refusal of the enemy to fulfil their assigned role caught D Company by surprise. The VC turned the tables on the Australians because the operation's planners had not considered the possibility that the enemy would behave in an unexpected manner. The VC also successfully negated Australian firepower by remaining in close contact. Consequently, neither the helicopter gunships hovering overhead nor the guns of 106 Battery were able to engage the enemy without the risk of hitting the Australian infantry. The plan's intelligence was also at fault. Instead of a rear echelon element, D Company assaulted the HQ Company of the *Chau Duc District Company*.

This was a well-armed, trained and experienced opponent. The camp also contained about 40 VC—double the expected number. The Australians gained the enemy's camp, but at the cost of 2 KIA and 22 WIA.

Fire Support Base Coral

During the Tet Offensive the task force deployed outside the borders of Phuoc Tuy into the adjoining Bien Hoa and Long Khanh provinces. Its task was to interdict VC operations in AO Columbus. In particular, the Australians were to prevent the enemy from launching rocket attacks against the huge American bases at Bien Hoa and Long Binh.

Gunners of 101 Field Battery fire their M2A2 105 mm gun in a night support mission. A cornerstone of Australian operations in Vietnam was the necessity to provide manoeuvring forces with immediate access to artillery support. AWM FAI/70/0169/VN.

Despite the failure of Tet, the VC continued to apply pressure in the Saigon region, in part to capitalise on the anti-war reaction that their offensive had occasioned in the United States. In April 1 ATF deployed once more outside Phuoc Tuy on Operation *Toan Thang I*. This operation saw the task force operate in a number of AOs from the Hat Dich area of Phuoc Tuy and extend into Bien Hoa Province in an arc north and north-east of Saigon. The task force's objective during this period was similar to its Tet mission. The Australians were to interdict the VC line of communication, intercept the movement of enemy units, and safeguard the approaches to Saigon and the American bases at Bien Hoa and Long Binh.

On the morning of 5 May the VC began their offensive. This round of attacks was neither as powerful nor as determined as Tet, and within a few days the VC disengaged and withdrew. HQ II FFV ordered Hughes to relocate 1 ATF further into Bien Hoa into an area the Australians designated AO Surfers. 1 ATF sub-divided Surfers into three battalion AOs called Bondi, Manly and Newport. The new Australian AO sat astride a major VC infiltration and supply route, and it had seen recent heavy use during the enemy's latest attack on Saigon.

On 12 May 1 ATF established FSB Coral in AO Bondi. It was not a smooth helicopter insertion. Air traffic control problems resulted in the piecemeal arrival of units, and some troops found themselves at alternate landing zones. HQ 1 ATF (Adv), HQ 1 RAR, Support Company 1 RAR, HQ 12 Field Regiment, and 102 Field Battery were all at Coral. 161 Field Battery RNZA ended up 1,000 metres to the south at its own temporary FSB. Rifle companies from 1 and 3 RAR deployed into their own AOs.

An American assisting the insertion warned, 'Charlie will come looking for you – you don't have to find him.' He was right. On the evening of the insertion, patrols from 1 RAR had two contacts. Early that morning, at 0145 hours, FSB Coral came under RPG and mortar bombardment. Shortly thereafter, a VC battalion stormed the perimeter, striking the sector defended by 1 RAR's mortar platoon and part of 102 Field Battery. The enemy approached so quickly that they breached the hastily laid wire and were among the mortars before 161 Field Battery RNZA could respond to a fire request. Within minutes the VC had overrun the mortars and captured one of 102 Field Battery's howitzers.

View of FSB Coral from the south-east.
AWM P01178.001.

The battle for Coral raged through the night. At several points the surviving mortar crewmen, who still clung to their position, received orders to get down while 102 Field Battery fired its guns at point blank range over their heads. Steel darts from splintex shells swept away anyone on the surface, while from above, six mini-guns of a Spooky aircraft flayed the ground. Helicopter gunships also arrived to aid the Australians. From the south the New Zealanders sent salvos of shells into the surrounding area, striking at possible enemy concentrations.

Despite the storm of shells the VC hung on, and did not break contact until 0800 hours. In the morning the Australians recovered the bodies of 52 VC. Their own losses were nine KIA and 28 WIA, 13 from the mortar platoon.

On 13 May the APCs of A Squadron 3 Cavalry Regiment arrived to bolster the garrison, and the infantry sent out patrols to locate the VC and take command of the ground. The rest of HQ 1 ATF (main) also arrived. At the same time 3 RAR moved into AO Manly to set up FSB Coogee. In addition, on 21 May the Centurion tanks of 1 Armoured Regiment received orders to move up to Coral. They arrived on 23 May.

FSB Coral as it appeared on 15 May. At this point the APCs had arrived and the Australians had implemented an integrated defence plan.
Mark Wahlert.

The events of the next few days showed that the Australian FSBs sat in a VC hot zone. Australian patrols fought frequent engagements with enemy parties. For example, on 14 May alone 1 RAR had the following contacts:

- 1200 hours: VC ambushed 12 Platoon resulting in 1 Aus KIA, 3 Aus WIA.
- 1253 hours: 5 Platoon engaged a group of VC, possibly wounding 2.
- 1630 hours: 2 Platoon fired on a group of 13 VC, causing the enemy to withdraw.
- 1700 hours: 7 Platoon located 9 VC and killed 7 and captured 2 at a cost to themselves of 1 KIA and 1 WIA.
- 1730 hours: VC killed 5 Platoon's lead scout in an ambush. The Australians reacted strongly, killing 4 VC but suffering 1 WIA.
- 1800 hours: a RPG round landed in A Company's position causing 2 WIA.

Despite 1 RAR's intensive patrolling, the VC were able to manoeuvre a regimental-strength force into a position to attack FSB Coral. They struck on the night of 15/16 May. At 0230 hours the enemy rocked the base with a heavy mortar and RPG bombardment. Under cover of this fire the enemy assaulted the perimeter guarded by A and B Companies 1 RAR. This time the defenders were more prepared. The infantry had had time to lay out fields of fire, the base headquarters had established communication links to all its units that allowed it to coordinate the defence, and the APCs had arrived to provide support. The mortar platoon also had a chance to fulfil its proper role and its four tubes fired 750 rounds during the attack. An hour later the VC broke contact, only to shift the attack to C Company's perimeter. The defenders also repulsed this challenge, just as they did a later strike on D Company. Before 0700 hours the enemy withdrew, pursued by Spooky and ground attack aircraft. Later that morning, patrols from 1 RAR located the enemy's mortar position. The counter-battery fire from 1 RAR's mortars had found their mark and the VC's position was heavily cratered.

Gunners of 12 Field Regiment man their positions on the perimeter at FSB Coral. Note the howitzer's depressed barrel. The gunners had repulsed an enemy assault on 13 May, firing over open sights.
AWM ERR/68/0515/VN.

The VC continued to operate in the area. On 17 May a patrol spotted a party of 35 enemy. The Australians directed gunfire onto their position resulting in 6 VC KIA.

On 24 May, 3 RAR abandoned FSB Coogee and established FSB Balmoral in AO Newport. The men of 3 RAR did not have to wait long for the VC to challenge their arrival. On 26 May the VC attempted to overrun Balmoral, but the assaulting waves broke when hit by concentrated canister fire from the tanks and the well-placed fire of D Company's soldiers. On 28 May the VC tried again with even less success, while FSB Coral came under another mortar barrage.

An operations officer leaves 1 ATF's underground command post at FSB Coral.
AWM HAL/68/0528/VN.

Dead VC litter a crater made by a bomb dropped from a B52 bomber.
The location is near FSB Balmoral.
AWM P02322.004.

During the day the Australians continued to push out patrols. Encounters with enemy parties and discoveries of bunker systems were frequent, and included a pitched battle between C Company 1 RAR and an enemy force of company strength. In this instance APCs and tanks from FSB Coral came to the infantry's aid. The Australians closed FSB Balmoral on 5 June and FSB Coral the next day. The task force then returned to Nui Dat. During *Toan Thang I* the Australians had suffered 25 KIA and 99 WIA, and inflicted on the enemy at least 276 KIA, 69 WIA, and 11 PW.

HUNTING THE VC

Search and Destroy

Westmoreland's strategy of attrition made search and destroy the most important type of operation for the Americans. Hence it was the mission that MACV prioritised in its efforts to defeat the VC. Search and destroy correlated with the US Army's concept of conventional war and, in accordance with its doctrine, MACV sought the destruction of the enemy's forces in a decisive battle. As a methodology of warfighting, search and destroy built upon American advantages in firepower, technology and logistics. It was not, however, a discriminating approach to warfighting, and its application posed great difficulties for the Americans, especially when it came to their ability to distinguish friend from foe. When the term 'search and destroy' fell out of favour, MACV substituted the more palatable name 'reconnaissance in force', although the nature of the mission did not change.

American search and destroy operations were not subtle. Instead they were large, loud, bold affairs that featured armadas of helicopters, seemingly unlimited air and artillery support, and convoys of vehicles. They began with confidence but generally ended in frustration. The critical difficulty facing the Americans in successfully implementing their strategy was that to destroy the VC they first had to locate them, and if a contact did occur they then had to compel the enemy to accept battle. It was only in the presence of such conditions that the Americans could bring to bear the massive firepower and technology superiorities that they possessed and use them to crush the VC. This happened rarely. VC units were difficult to find and, once found, they were even harder to fix.

Lesson 13

Whether you are conducting a major offensive or a small patrol, noise will alert the enemy to your strength and intentions, and they will use this information to your disadvantage.

Complicating the implementation of search and destroy operations was the fact that the advantages which the United States sought to bring to bear against the VC—namely mobility, firepower and technology—provided the VC with the means to avoid contact. As one Australian observer commented, 'the use of helicopters for troop insertion, along with long fire preparation of LZs made surprise impossible.' MACV's procedures were noisy and large scale and these invariably tipped off the VC as to its intentions.

As 1 ATF was subordinate to II FFV, large-scale search and destroy missions were also an important mission for the Australians. On numerous occasions II FFV planned operations for Phuoc Tuy and tasked the Australians to participate. One such instance was Operation *Toledo* after the Battle of Long Tan. A post-operation analysis summarised the Australian experience: 'the enemy were able to fade away from the large scale heliborne assaults and to reassemble in the same area after the assault force was lifted elsewhere... The operation was not successful in destroying main force elements...'. Operation *Toledo*'s main accomplishment was against the enemy's support structure. The allies destroyed over twenty base camps and captured more than 127,000 rounds of small arms ammunition, 660 mortar bombs and 185 tons of rice.

Another typical large-scale operation was *Paddington* which commenced in July 1967. It involved most of 1 ATF including: 2 RAR, 7 RAR, A Sqn 3 Cavalry Regiment, 4 Field Regiment and 1 Field Squadron. The American contribution was 1 Brigade 9 Infantry Division, 11 Armoured Cavalry Regiment, as well as supporting artillery and air assets. Two South Vietnamese Marine battalions also participated. The American commitment was colossal, as 11 Cavalry's designation as an armoured regiment was misleading. In fact, its establishment contained over 1,300 AFVs.

Operation *Paddington* took place just north of the village of Xuyen Moc in eastern Phuoc Tuy. Its objective was the destruction of *HQ 5 VC Division* and its subordinate *275 VC Regiment*. The operation called for 1 ATF to establish a blocking position onto which the cavalry would drive the VC. This was the standard tactical solution to the difficult problems of finding and trapping an elusive enemy. In essence, the task of the manoeuvre element of the attacking force was to flush out the VC as if they were a flock of quail and drive the enemy towards a line of shooters. The blocking force would engage the approaching VC and fix them on the killing ground. Now encircled, the enemy would be crushed between the manoeuvre and blocking forces. This tactic was also described as 'hammer and anvil'.

The VC response to hammer and anvil tactics was for their units to break up into small parties which could slip through the inevitable holes in the encircling net. Due to the difficulty of the terrain and the density of the jungle the VC needed only minute gaps in the hunting force's ranks to evade danger. Once through the allied line the insurgents re-formed in a different area. When the operation ended and the allied forces redeployed for a new task the VC could reoccupy the sector from which they had moved.

This is precisely what happened in Operation *Paddington*: the VC slipped the net and made good their escape. The operation was not without benefit to the Americans and Australians. The allied force killed 31 VC and discovered several VC base camps that they subsequently destroyed. However, it must be admitted that Operation *Paddington* failed to achieve its primary objective; *HQ 5 VC Division* and *275 VC Regiment* remained alive and continued to irritate the allies and prey upon the province's villagers.

There was another factor that contributed to the overall failure of search and destroy operations to achieve their objective. American and Australian commanders and planners confused the ability to launch an operation with that of having the initiative to decide when and where battle would occur. To launch an operation and to retain the initiative are not the same. The reality of combat in Vietnam was that allied forces could commence operations at will, and did so, but it was the VC who determined whether or not battle would take place. This is why so many allied search and destroy missions ended without the desired result—the VC refused to give battle. In Vietnam it was the insurgents who held the initiative and in most cases it was they, not the allies, who decided when and where battle would take place. Post-activity reports supported this conclusion as they showed that it was the VC who commenced 88 per cent of contacts. For the most part, when faced by a superior force, the nimble VC declined obliteration and slipped away.

In Phuoc Tuy, 1 ATF organised numerous search and destroy operations of its own. While smaller than those assembled by II FFV, their objective was the same: the destruction of local VC

Lesson 14

In general, search and destroy operations involving large allied forces return poor rewards relative to the investment of men and material required. One problem with this type of counter-insurgency mission is that the scale of the operation is often so disproportionately large, compared to the enemy's strength, that it encourages the enemy to avoid combat rather than risk obvious annihilation by a much more powerful force. Vastly superior technological, logistic and firepower advantages can hinder rather than facilitate contact and encourage the enemy to seek asymmetric alternatives rather than direct confrontation.

Lesson 15

Battle is guaranteed only if the enemy has no choice but to accept combat. Operations that cannot impose this prerequisite will often end in failure.

units. The result was the same for the Australians as it was for the Americans. Contacts were frequent, and Australian and VC soldiers lost their lives, but the combat was not of a decisive nature.

The pattern for Australian search and destroy missions was set soon after the task force began operating in Phuoc Tuy. 6 RAR conducted Operation *Ingham* from 18 November to 3 December 1966. The battalion's historian described the experience as:

> a multitude of contacts with small groups of Viet Cong, by all companies. The larger [VC] forces had withdrawn, the smaller caretaker members of the enemy using delaying tactics such as Claymore mines and booby traps, to slow down the battalion's advance and cover their own withdrawal ... Mines were a constant hazard ...

RPD 7.62mm LMG (USSR) & Chicom Type 56 LMG (PRC)

Calibre: 7.62 mm
Operation:
  Gas, belt fed, automatic fire
Length: 1837 mm
Weight: 7.4 kg empty
Muzzle velocity: 753 m/sec
Feeding: 100 rounds in drum
Rate of fire: 650 rpm
Effective range: 800 m

The RPD (*Ruchnoy Pulemet Degtyarova*) was one of the most common LMGs in use by the VC during the Vietnam War. It first appeared in the Second World War and remained the Soviet Army's standard squad automatic weapon until the 1960s. More common among the VC was the Chinese variant, the Type 56 LMG. Both weapons were light and simple to use. They fired a 7.62mm round from a 100-round belt that was contained in a drum mounted below the gun. The RPD provided effective firepower up to a range of 800 metres.

A Russian made RPD (Ruchnoy Pulemet Degtyarova) light machine-gun that 1 RAR captured from the VC. RAICM.

Close-up of detail of RPD feed mechanism. RAICM.

Similarly, in July 1969 patrols from 4 RAR/NZ (ANZAC) discovered a major VC base system in the Hat Dich area during Operation *Merino*. However, by the time the battalion was in position to attack—two nights later— the enemy had vanished. 6 RAR's and 4 RAR/NZ (ANZAC)'s experiences on Operations *Ingham* and *Merino* suggest the weakness of search and destroy missions to 'find, fix and finish' the VC. These were dangerous missions in which the Australians made contact, took casualties in brief and furious firefights, and ran the risk of mines and booby traps, but in each of these cases the target of the operation made good its escape.

When the Australians did manage to bring the enemy to battle during a search and destroy operation it was generally against a VC rearguard party that sacrificed itself in order to allow the main body to escape. One example of this was the Battle of Suoi Chau Pha. It took place on 6 August 1967 during Operation *Ballarat*, and involved A Company 7 RAR against elements of *274 VC Regiment*. At approximately 1040 hours members of 2 Platoon discovered fresh VC tracks near the Suoi Chau Pha Creek, the feature from which the battle takes its name. A Company's commander, Major Ewart O'Donnell, ordered 2 Platoon to follow the tracks.

The platoon had not gone far when its lead scout spotted two VC moving towards them down the trail. Using hand signals the scout alerted the rest of the platoon which took up an ambush position. Moments later, when the VC had entered the killing zone, the Australians opened up and fire tore into both insurgents.

At the precise moment that 2 Platoon cut down its two careless victims it was not possible for O'Donnell to know whether this was an isolated encounter or whether the two VC were members of a nearby enemy force. In this instance it turned out to be the latter. 2 Platoon's brief encounter with the two insurgents quickly escalated into a fierce firefight that lasted two hours and involved all of A Company.

From the Australian side, the battle developed almost as a drill. As soon as 2 Platoon made contact the company's FO, Lieutenant Neville Clark, alerted 106 Field Battery, 7 RAR's designated support battery. Clark brought shells onto the track and further back in the direction from whence the VC approached. The idea was that if the two dead insurgents were a VC column's scouts the barrage would catch additional enemy before they could take cover.

As 105 mm shells exploded, O'Donnell ordered 2 Platoon to advance and probe for a possible enemy position. The platoon had not gone far when it walked into a hail of machine-gun and RPG fire; within moments the platoon's commander and platoon sergeant were hit. O'Donnell reacted by ordering 1 Platoon to sweep around to the right, find the enemy's flank, get behind the VC and relieve the pressure on 2 Platoon. Once again heavy RGP and automatic weapon fire found the manoeuvring Australians, and 1 Platoon took heavy casualties, including two section commanders dead and a dozen wounded.

The battle developed into a fierce fight at close range between two evenly matched bodies of infantry. The VC brought into action seven machine-guns against the Australians' six, and to the diggers it appeared as if every VC carried an AK47. The difference in the strength of the two sides lay in the Australian artillery. Clark continued to pour shells down behind the VC and walk them back through the enemy's positions. Clark also ordered into the fight the 155 mm guns of 'A' Battery 2/35 Artillery Battalion, the American gunners attached to 1 ATF at Nui Dat. Accessing the II FFV artillery net, Clark brought American 8 inch and 175 mm guns into play. Over the course of the battle the gunners fired over 1200 rounds.

Despite the gunners' efforts the VC negated much of the Australian firepower by hugging A Company's positions. This tactic also exploited a weakness in the Australian infantry's weapon mix. As a close support weapon the Australians relied on the M79. However, the battle was fought at such close range that many of the 40 mm rounds that the Australians fired failed to explode because they did not travel far enough to arm. Those that did arm had a tendency to detonate from striking a leaf instead of the intended target. The VC RPGs did not suffer from this liability. Consequently, rocket grenade explosions rocked Australian positions throughout the action.

M79 40mm Grenade Launcher (USA)

Calibre: 40 mm
Operation:
single shot, break open, hand fed
Length: 736 mm
Weight:
2.7 kg empty, 2.92 kg loaded
Rate of fire: up to 4 rpm
Muzzle Velocity: 76 m/sec
Range:
400 m maximum

Nicknamed 'Wombat Gun' by Australian soldiers in Vietnam, the M79 closely resembled a large bore, single barrel, sawn-off shotgun. It fired a 40mm HE grenade, although smoke and illumination rounds were also available. Flechette and buckshot rounds appeared later in the war. The M79 covered the zone between the throwing distance of a hand grenade and the lowest range of the 81mm mortar.

The M79.
RAICM.

A captured RPG7 is examined by Privates J. Ward and Mick King.
The weapon has an optical sight attached.
AWM THU/68/0264/VN.

An RPG7 with rocket. The RPG7 could penetrate APC and Centurion Tank armour.
RAICM.

An RPG2 with rocket.
RAICM

RPG7 Light Anti-tank Rocket Launcher (USSR) & Chicom Type 69 (PRC)

Calibre: 40 mm
Operation:
  recoilless, shoulder fired; muzzle loaded; re-loadable smoothbore rocket grenade launcher
Length: 953 mm
Weight:
  7.9 kg launcher; 2.25 kg grenade
Range: 300–500 m

The RPG7 was introduced into the Soviet forces in 1961, and copied by China as the Type 69. In Vietnam it was an upgrade of the less effective RPG2, although the older weapon remained in service. The RPG7 was a short-range, muzzle-loaded, shoulder-fired, anti-tank, rocket-propelled grenade that the VC employed against Australian armour and defensive positions. The RPG7 grenade was capable of penetrating the hull of the Centurion tank and the M113A1 APC, and when detonated against trees produced a hail of splinters that made it into a dangerous anti-personnel weapon. Simple to operate and inexpensive to produce, the RPG7 was one of the most successful anti-tank weapons yet seen.

M203 40mm Under-Barrel Grenade Launcher (USA)

Calibre: 40 mm
Operation:
  single shot, pump action, hand fed
Length: 385 mm
Weight:
  4.8 kg empty, 5.45 kg loaded
Rate of fire: up to 4 rpm
Muzzle velocity: 72 m/sec
Range:
  400 m maximum

The M203 is a light-weight, compact, breech-loading, pump-action, single shot grenade launcher that attached to the underside of the M16 rifle. It was an upgrade of the M79, and was introduced into service in late 1970, but never entirely replaced the M79.

The M203 attached to the M16 rifle. RAICM.

As Australian casualties mounted, the dust-off choppers of 9 RAAF Squadron arrived. The helicopters flew into heavy fire, and one was put out of action with its pilot and onboard medic hit. Despite the fire, the RAAF pilots continued to fly in to A Company's position to lift off the wounded. 7 RAR also used helicopters to insert B Company in a blocking position but they made no further contact with the enemy once the battle ended.

Neither side was able to gain the upper hand and after two hours the VC broke off. The next day 7 RAR discovered a battalion-size VC base camp. Presumably the VC that A Company fought were a rearguard who sacrificed themselves to allow the main force time to escape.

Lesson 16

The enemy will identify patterns in your tactics. Therefore, it is essential that commanders vary their methods in order not to signal their intentions. If tactics become stereotyped the enemy will make you pay.

The Battle of Suoi Chau Pha confirmed the lesson on the value of firepower that the Australians had learned the previous year at Long Tan. The Australian infantry had immediate access to significant artillery resources in case of a contact. A Company training also allowed its men to respond almost instinctively to a chance meeting. However the enemy's anticipation of A Company's reactions highlighted the need for the Australians to vary their tactics. Well-prepared and heavily armed VC savaged first 2 Platoon, as it probed along the track, and then 1 Platoon when it sought out the enemy's flank. The platoons initiated well-drilled procedures, but ones which the enemy had learned and to which they had adapted.

The Australians rarely forced the VC to fight a major battle in Phuoc Tuy, despite the considerable manpower and other resources at their disposal. Battles such as Long Tan were not the result of a search and destroy mission; it was the VC who brought

105

about the action. Other major battles in Phuoc Tuy were also the result of VC initiative, including the seizure of Ba Ria during the Tet Offensive in 1968 and the Battle of Binh Ba in 1969. As they did elsewhere in South Vietnam, communist forces in Phuoc Tuy held the initiative and it was the insurgents who decided when, where and if battle would take place.

Over the course of the conflict in Phuoc Tuy the Australians did succeed in weakening the VC field forces, but they were unable to destroy them. When the Australians handed the province over to the ARVN in 1971 the VC organisation remained intact.

'Dustoff'. This scene represents a typical medical evacuation. A Huey hovers overhead to winch a wounded digger to safety, as other soldiers form a defensive ring on the ground. VC fire reaches up into the sky. At more secure LZs the helicopter would have landed. Gouache on board.
Jeff Isaacs, OAM.

Operation *Pinnaroo*

One of the insurgency's most important base areas in Phuoc Tuy was the Long Hai Hills. While the feature's peak was only 327 metres in height it was formidable terrain; the jungle-clad hills were extremely steep and rugged, and riddled with limestone caves. The communists, who called the area the Minh Dam Secret Zone, had established themselves in the Long Hai Hills during the Second World War. By the time of the Australians' arrival they had converted the area into a major base and logistic centre. It was home to *C25 Long Dat District Company*, the *Vung Tau Guerrilla Platoon*, and often a company from *D445 Provincial Mobile Battalion*. It also provided sanctuary for numerous logistic and administrative units including district headquarters. From their bases in these hills the VC were within easy striking distance of the province's main population centres and the allied logistic establishment at Vung Tau.

Private Graham Taylor, 3 RAR, sights a Russian rifle captured during Operation *Pinnaroo*. The Australians found the rifle in an underground hospital complex.
AWM CRO/68/3009/VN.

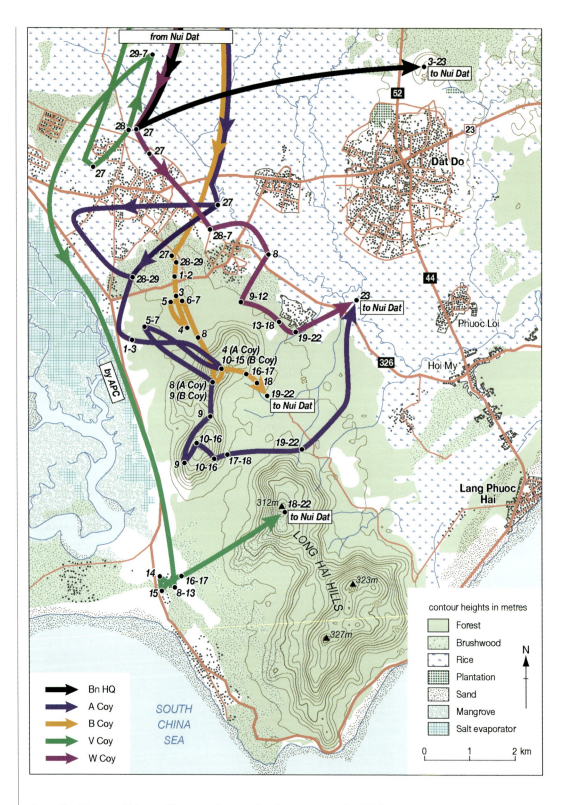

from Nui Dat

29-7

3-23 to Nui Dat

52

23

28

27

27

27

27

Dat Do

28-7

8

27   28-29

1-2

5   3
    6-7

44

9-12

13-18

23 **to Nui Dat**

19-22

Phuoc Loi

5-7

4   8

1-3

28-29

4 (A Coy)
10-15 (B Coy)

16-17
18

19-22
to Nui Dat

326

Hoi My

8 (A Coy)
9 (B Coy)

9

10-16

19-22

by APC

9   10-16   17-18

19-22

**Lang Phuoc
Hai**

312m   18-22
to Nui Dat

LONG HAI HILLS

323m

14   16-17

15   8-13

327m

contour heights in metres

	Forest
	Brushwood
	Rice
	Plantation
	Sand
	Mangrove
	Salt evaporator

N

*SOUTH
CHINA
SEA*

➤ Bn HQ

➤ A Coy

➤ B Coy

➤ V Coy

➤ W Coy

0   1   2 km

Operation *Pinnaroo*. This map illustrates the convoluted movements of 2 RAR/NZ.
Not shown are 3 RAR's routes. Its AO was the southern sector of the Long Hai Hills.
Kay Dancey.

The Long Hai Hills were a thorn in the side of the Australians. In February 1968 Hughes organised Operation *Pinnaroo*, a search and destroy mission to deal with the enemy in their refuge. *Pinnaroo* was a major undertaking for 1 ATF, and Hughes allocated to it most of the task force's strength including 2 RAR/NZ, 3 RAR, C Squadron 1 Armoured Regiment, A Squadron 3 Cavalry Regiment, 4 Field Regiment, 1 Field Squadron and 9 Squadron RAAF. In addition, the Australians had the support of two American batteries and an army aviation company. This was not the Australians' first visit to the Long Hai Hills. In February 1967 during Operation *Renmark* 5 RAR had swept through the feature, and the American 173 Airborne Brigade (Separate) had cleared the hills prior to 1 ATF's deployment.

Hughes had one advantage that convinced him that the time was ripe to clear the Long Hai Hills and thereby relieve the communists' pressure on the nearby villages. The task force enjoyed excellent intelligence in the lead-up to Operation *Pinnaroo*. On 28 January 1968 a communist deserter surrendered to provincial authorities in Ba Ria. He had spent two years in the Long Hai Hills and provided the Australians with the location of VC base camps, caves and minefields. He also told the Australians that the area contained between 1000 and 2000 insurgents, nearly all of them armed.

Operation *Pinnaroo* commenced on 27 February 1968 and lasted for more than six weeks ending on 15 April. Each battalion began the operation by establishing blocking positions in order to trap the VC inside the hill line. In the next stage the infantry began a slow but steady penetration into the feature, supported by APCs and tanks. Hourly progress was measured in metres; the Australians advanced slowly because the enemy based their defence on mines and booby traps and had sown the devices thickly throughout the area.

At no point during Operation *Pinnaroo* did the Australians succeed in trapping the VC in what could be termed a 'conventional' battle. Instead, they had a number of brief contacts and ambushes, interspersed by long periods of slow, careful patrolling. Table 3 outlines the contacts obtained by 3 RAR and its supporting arms.

During Operation *Pinnaroo* 3 RAR suffered 25 casualties. As Table 3 suggests very few of these were the result of enemy fire. Instead, nearly all were caused by the enemy's mines and booby traps. 2 RAR/NZ also incurred most of its losses from these devices. On 1 March, ten 2 RAR/NZ soldiers were wounded in two mine incidents.

TABLE 3
3 RAR Contacts during Operation Pinnaroo

Time	Sub Unit	Details	Result
9 March, 0920 hrs	2/A/3 Cav	APC hit by RPG 7	1 AUS WIA, 1 ARVN WIA
10 March, 2030 hrs	5/B/3 RAR	Contact with 3 VC	1 pair bloody thongs found
13 March, 2152 hrs	8/C/3 RAR	Contact with 8-10 VC	4 VC KIA
14 March, 1045 hrs	7/C/3 RAR	Contact with 1 VC	Unknown
15 March, 1115 hrs	2/A/3 RAR	Contact with approximately 10 VC	1 VC KIA
18 March, 2315 hrs	6/B/3 RAR	Contact with 1 VC	Unknown
20 March, 1025 hrs	6/B/3 RAR	Came under fire by VC LMG and AK47 fire	1 VC KIA 1 AUS KIA
21 March, 1942 hrs	D/3 RAR	Ambush VC force of section strength	4 VC KIA
23 March, 1015 hrs	AT Pl 3 RAR	Contact with 1 VC	1 VC detained
23 March, 1639 hrs	C/3 RAR	Sighted 1 VC	VC disappeared into a cave and escaped
26 March, 0320 hrs	D/3 RAR	Contact with 2 VC	1 VC WIA and taken POW
26 March, 1020 hrs	D/3 RAR	Contact with 6 VC	2 VC KIA
26 March, 1220 hrs	C/3 RAR	Contact with 1 VC	1 VC KIA
26 March, 1530 hrs	C/3 RAR	Contact with 1 VC	1 VC POW
26 March, 2155 hrs	C/3 RAR	Ambush party of VC	2 VC WIA and taken
29 March, 0835 hrs	C/3 RAR	Contact with 4 VC	4 VC POW
31 March, 0745 hrs	C Sqn 1 Arm Regt	Capture 1 VC	1 VC POW
5 April, 1250 hrs	C/3 RAR	1 Fd Sqn search cave and come under fire by unknown number of VC	1 Aus DOW
7 April, 1740 hrs	9/C/3 RAR	Contact with 3 VC	1 VC KIA
11 April, 0510 hrs	AT Pl 3 RAR	Ambush 2 VC	1 VC KIA 1 VC WIA
11 April, 1450 hrs	12/D/3 RAR	Contact with 5-6 VC	1 VC KIA

3 RAR Contacts during Operation *Pinnaroo*. The table highlights the relative infrequency and small scale of the battalion's contacts. Most of the VC in the Long Hai Hills avoided the Australian sweep.
Mark Wahlert.

Hughes understood the threat the enemy's mines posed when he planned the operation and took steps to reduce the danger, although he knew it was impossible to eliminate the risk. To increase anti-mine capabilities, the infantry battalions brigaded their pioneers with the sappers of 1 Field Squadron from whom they received mine removal training. Formed into clearance teams of one engineer and one pioneer, they preceded the infantry, searching for mines and booby traps. The infantry, in turn, provided cover for the clearance teams. To assist, the field squadron doubled its normal allocation of mine detectors to 96. Teams worked for no longer than an hour, then another team took over to continue the measured advance which averaged only 50 metres an hour. Hughes was so concerned that he arranged for either five or six B-52 strikes in front of 3 RAR's route into the hills near Phuoc Long. While the planes targeted VC positions, he also hoped that the exploding bombs would detonate the VC's minefields.

The engineers assisted in another role too—the destruction of the enemy's camp and cave systems. During Operation *Pinnaroo* the sappers employed 2,500 pounds of TNT, 26,000 pounds of C4 and over 38,500 pounds of beehive-shaped charges. On 28 March, for example, 1 Field Squadron destroyed a multi-level cave complex that contained connecting ladders and a supply of fresh water.

Operation *Pinnaroo*'s casualty toll was almost equally divided between the two sides:

- Australian: 10 KIA, 25 WIA (including 11 NZ)
- VC: 21 KIA, 5 WIA, 4 POW, 34 detainees

In addition, the Australians captured nearly 100 individual and crew-served weapons, ammunition and 2.5 tons of rice, and destroyed 57 camps and bunker systems.

At the operation's conclusion the Australians considered the Long Hai Hills cleared. Indeed, it was a major accomplishment to have penetrated the enemy's redoubt and to have raised the Australian flag over these hills. Moreover, the diggers had forced the enemy from one of their most important redoubts. At the end of the operation Hughes pulled the Australians out and handed the area's protection to the Provincial Chief. Hughes explained afterwards that, 'I couldn't just have troops sitting round doing that – my troops were of better quality than pure garrison troops.' Soon thereafter the South Vietnamese troops also pulled out, handing the Long Hai Hills back to the enemy.

Lance Corporal David Halliday (l) and Private John Scott (r) raise the
Australian Flag over the Long Hai Hills during Operation *Pinnaroo*.
AWM THU/68/0273/VN.

Operation *Pinnaroo*'s success proved fleeting. When the operation
commenced the Australians estimated that there were more than
1000 communists in the Long Hai Hills. During *Pinnaroo* the
Australians accounted for 64 VC. The anomaly between the two
figures is due to the fact that most of the VC left the Long Hai
Hills when it became clear that the Australians were coming.
B-52 strikes, while an impressive display of firepower, gave the
enemy clear warning of the seriousness of the Australian intent;
the United States Air Force did not allocate these aircraft lightly.
Hughes was aware that the VC had dispersed and admitted that
he did not have enough troops to cordon the whole area. As so
often happened, the VC found the gaps in the Australian screen
and eluded the task force. It also became evident that the VC
had many more caves than the Australians found. The result was
that within months the VC had reoccupied the Long Hai Hills
and resumed operations.

Cordon and Search

Cordon and search was the task force's second major method of hunting the VC. However, instead of sweeps through the jungle to destroy the VC's units, the target of cordon and search missions was the insurgency's village infrastructure, cadres and sympathisers. Cordon and search is a combined military-civil mission that involves agencies of the local government and the police. The military's role is to plan the operation, provide troops for the cordon, escort police search parties, protect government officials, and guard detainees. The military is also responsible for the operation's security including the elimination or capture of guerrillas found inside the village, and the provision of protection against insurgents attacking from outside the cordon.

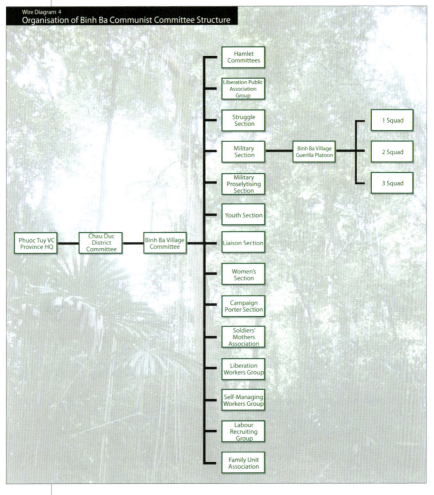

Wire Diagram 4
Organisation of Binh Ba Communist Committee Structure

Wire Diagram 4 demonstrates the extent of the VC organisation found in Phuoc Tuy's villages. The VC had created committees that penetrated all aspects of village life. The diagram also shows that the military component of the VC village structure represented a minor part of the entire organisation.
Mark Wahlert.

Operation *Holsworthy*, which ran from 5 to 18 August 1966, was the task force's first cordon and search mission in Phuoc Tuy. Its target was Binh Ba, a large village of 1500 inhabitants, and the nearby satellite hamlets of Duc Trung (population 600) and Duc My (population 200). The three villages served as housing and processing plant for the adjacent Gallia Rubber Plantation, and they lay next to Route 2 north of the Australian base at Nui Dat. The plantation still operated, but only because its French managers collaborated with the VC. In return for tax payments and supplies of rice and other foodstuffs, the VC permitted the French managers to continue to tap rubber.

As a result of their arrangement with the plantation's managers, the VC had a strong presence in Binh Ba; the town contained an extensive network of support committees and an active guerrilla platoon. Intelligence reports estimated that 20 per cent of Binh Ba's population were either active VC or supporters of the insurgency. Wire Diagram 4 outlines the communists' structure in Binh Ba.

Cordon and search missions are manpower-intensive operations. The participating troops need sufficient strength to establish the cordon and to search the village, while retaining sufficient numbers to deter possible enemy attempts to disrupt the operation. Cordon and search operations also require the same access to supporting arms—artillery, mine removal, gunship, and medical evacuation—that search and destroy missions need. The Australian Commander, Jackson, allocated to the search of Binh Ba nearly all of the task force's strength, including:

- 5 RAR
- C & D Company 6 RAR
- 1 APC Squadron (-)
- 105 Field Battery
- Battery 'A' 2/35 Artillery (US)
- 1 Troop 1 Field Squadron
- 1 ATF Linguist Section (det)
- One Medcap Team
- section 1 Transport Platoon
- Psyops detachment
- one FAC Radio Operator
- one H13, 161 (Ind) Recce Flight
- one HU1B, 9 Squadron RAAF
- one light fire team (US)
- one psyops voice aircraft (US)
- six Vietnamese police officers

The operation was under command of Lieutenant-Colonel John Warr, the CO of 5 RAR.

Lieutenant John Hartley, 5 RAR, and two interpreters question a woman during Operation *Holsworthy*.
AWM FOR/66/0646/VN.

On the evening of 8 August, the infantry of 5 and 6 RAR secretly established themselves in harbours near Binh Ba and Duc Trung. In the small hours of 9 August the companies moved out in order to establish the cordon by 0530 hours. D Company 5 RAR and D Company 6 RAR surrounded Duc Trung while the rest of 5 RAR with C Company 6 RAR established a perimeter around Binh Ba. The belief was that if the Australians surrounded the villages before dawn they would trap any VC who happened to have returned home for the night.

Shortly after 0600 hours the villagers were awakened by the sound of the American psyops (psychological operations) aircraft buzzing overhead and the noise of approaching Australian APCs. The infantry then closed up, sealing the village. At the same time A Company 5 RAR, the battalion's anti-tank platoon, and sections of APCs set up road blocks on Route 2 and ambushes on likely approaches through the rubber trees as a precaution against VC intervention.

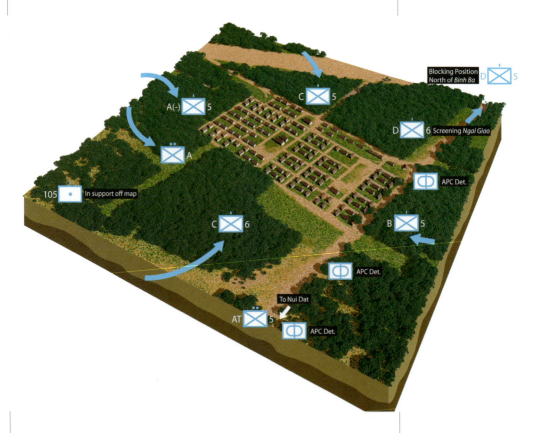

The Australian infantry close up and cordon Binh Ba prior to the commencement of the search. The illustration highlights the large number of troops needed to establish a tight cordon.
Mark Wahlert.

At 0730 hours the search of the villages commenced. Teams moved house-to-house, followed by a Medcap party to treat any sick that the investigation revealed. Each search team consisted of a section of infantry as a protection party, a team of four engineers in case of booby traps, an interpreter and a policeman. The teams moved methodically through the village, but it was a slow process. At 1500 hours Jackson and the Provincial Chief, Colonel Duc Dat, arrived. Dat addressed the assembled villagers and then began a hand-out of rice.

At the conclusion of the search of Duc Trung the troops employed there redeployed to Duc My and moved through that village. Due to the size of Binh Ba the Australians did not finish their search until 1000 hours on 10 August.

Soldiers of 5 RAR (Privates Bill Winkel (l) and Brian Ticknell (r)) examine
documents seized during Operation *Holsworthy*.
AWM FOR/66/0642/VN.

The objective of the search was to hold for questioning all males of VC military age (12 to 45 years), as well as to identify other communist supporters. Intelligence reports estimated that there were approximately 450 males in that age cohort in the three villages. As the search teams brought out the men the Australians moved them by APC to a temporary compound near the plantation's airstrip. After questioning, those identified as suspects were transferred to Ba Ria for further investigation by provincial authorities.

Over the next few days 5 RAR patrols reached out of Binh Ba, extending the task force's control over the area. As the villagers became comfortable with the Australians, the diggers received invitations for social visits to people's homes and played soccer with the children. The Medcap team was also busy. Over eight days they saw approximately 1200 patients. The villagers' main problems were vitamin and iron deficiencies due to a repetitive diet that lacked fresh fruit, vegetables and meat. In addition, 10 per cent of the local people tested positive for tuberculosis.

The cordon and search of Binh Ba not only brought the village back under the government's control but also allowed its people to rejoin the province. In the days after the operation over 500 villagers made the trip south on Route 2 to Ba Ria, enjoying their first opportunity since the VC's occupation to sell their produce at the provincial capital's markets and to buy goods for themselves. Militarily, Operation *Holsworthy* was a complete success. The Australians had wiped out the *Binh Ba Guerrilla Platoon*, and detained a further 77 villagers for questioning as possible VC members or sympathisers. The cost to the Australians was just three WIA, which represented an impressive positive cost ratio when compared to the number of casualties incurred on typical search and destroy missions. Afterwards Warr observed that the operation's effectiveness was greater than any previously undertaken by his battalion.

The task force continued to undertake cordon and search operations but they were never as numerous as search and destroy missions. Binh Ba did not stay VC-free for long. By October 1966 a VC cadre and guerrilla platoon were again in residence, and the collection of taxes and recruitment of insurgents had resumed. VC main force units had also become active to the north of Binh Ba. The task force's response was Operation *Caloundra* in January 1967, during which 5 RAR again cleaned out the village.

The reasons for the inability of the Australians to keep Binh Ba and other villages clear of VC were numerous, and included:

- the need to redeploy the task force onto other operations;
- a military preference for search and destroy operations;

- the technological imperative to maintain a high tempo of operations; and
- a reluctance to utilise the task force's highly skilled troops in static garrison roles.

Another factor was that the Australians had no responsibility for village defence. The protection of the people was technically the job of the South Vietnamese.

Civic Action

Australia's Civic Action program in Vietnam called for the use of the task force's resources to provide Phuoc Tuy's villagers with construction, logistic, educational, medical and dental assistance. The Civic Action program had multiple objectives, including:

- to gain the respect of the local people for Australian forces;
- to win over the villagers' hearts and minds;
- to improve the population's loyalty to the GVN;
- to enhance the people's health, well-being, and living conditions; and
- to strengthen the province's economic activity.

Civic action built on the improved security environment that resulted from the removal of insurgents after the completion of a cordon and search operation.

The task force had one further motivation for undertaking military civic action. The Australians believed that if they garnered the goodwill of the people of Phuoc Tuy it would increase their access to local intelligence. A civic action officer, Major W. P. Smith, explained that, 'the population, particularly in counter insurgency warfare, are perhaps one of the best sources of information. Most of the VC have relatives, a lot of the population know exactly what their relatives are doing.'

By the middle of 1971, 24 of Phuoc Tuy's villages had received construction assistance under Australia's Civic Action program. For example, the Australians provided Dat Do's high school students with a library and science block, Binh Gia's villagers gained a market, and Long Dien's children a youth and sports centre. In addition, medical and dental teams had made numerous visits across the provinces either as a part of a cordon and search operation or as a separate action. In a statement to Parliament on 24 February 1971, the Minister for Defence, John Malcolm Fraser, announced that the civic action program had resulted in the construction of six dispensaries, 71 classrooms, four community centres, 17 playgrounds, water supply enhancements to 14 villages, and treatment for 200,000 medical and 100,000 dental patients.

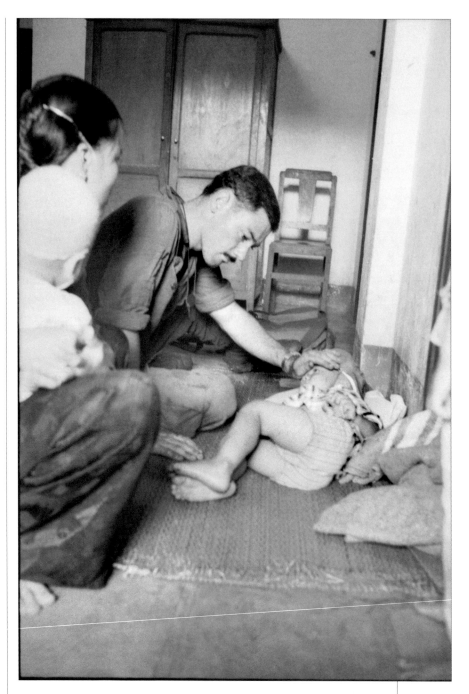

Stretcher Bearer Private Bill McIntyre, 5 RAR, assists a child in Binh Ba during Operation *Holsworthy*.
AWM FOR/66/0641/VN.

1 ATF engineers also participated in an American-sponsored lines of communication improvement program. The Australians rebuilt several of the province's main roads including: Route 2 from Ba Ria to the northern border; Route 44 from Ba Ria to Long Hai; and Route 23 from Dat Do to Xuyen Moc.

Despite an impressive list of achievements, much of 1 ATF's civic action program was marked by naïveté and heavy handedness on the part of the Australians, especially in the first half of the deployment. Once they were installed at Nui Dat, military civic action became an additional duty undertaken whenever time permitted and initiated by units themselves. The soldiers undertook projects for which they had the skills and that they could complete with the limited opportunity that their other duties allowed. Consultation to identify the needs of the villagers was either too brief or non-existent. In June 1968, 1 Australian Civil Affairs Unit arrived in Phuoc Tuy to take over direction of the task force's civic action program. The raising of this 40-man unit dedicated to civic action allowed the Australians to better target their efforts, but the task force's approach remained overly prescriptive.

Lesson 17

Ownership and consultation are critical factors in any civic action commitment. Military forces must provide what the local people actually want and need if a civic action program is to achieve its wider goals.

Australian civic action initiatives suffered from several core problems that reduced their benefit to Phuoc Tuy's peasants and minimized the advantages that accrued to the task force and the GVN. The undertaking of building projects without reference to the local people meant that villagers had no stake in the completed structure. The villagers neither built the facility nor owned it, and once completed there was no guarantee that it matched the needs or desires of the people. Furthermore, the Australians did not provide ongoing staff and materials. Maintenance and sustainment were the responsibility of the provincial government which did not necessarily have appropriately trained personnel, equipment and stores, or even the desire to take on an additional commitment. In addition, in setting up the program the Australians did not understand the central role of local government bodies at the hamlet, village and district levels in Vietnamese decision-making and failed to consult with these bodies. It was not until the advent of Vietnamisation in 1969 that involving villagers in the determination of projects, and in their construction, became a priority.

Australia's medical and dental civic action programs also had unanticipated negative effects. Medical support had the potential to be a life-saving intervention. However in such cases any benefit that accrued was limited to the individual saved and there was little flow-on to the GVN as a whole. In fact, Australian medical civic action tended to undercut the South Vietnamese government's efforts to provide for the care of its citizens. For example, an Australian pharmacist who visited a village was better stocked and more generous than the local GVN dispensary. This resulted in a cycle of dependency and expectation among villagers who waited for the arrival of Australian medical staff rather than visit a government pharmacy. In this manner medical civic action actually weakened instead of strengthening the local population's affiliation to its government.

In addition, medical and dental actions were never the primary mission of Australia's staff. Their skill lay in the treatment of young men injured in war not the caring for the ills of women and children. Ultimately, the first loyalty of Australian medical staff was to 1 ATF's soldiers, and Phuoc Tuy's villagers received attention only when conditions permitted. Therefore, the Australians were unable to provide continuous care, and if military action escalated the medical staff returned to their primary duties. In fact, medical civic action had to be managed carefully because the sudden removal of staff could signal to the insurgents the imminent commencement of an operation.

A senior ARVN officer summarised the basic problem of allied civic action that sponsoring forces struggled but usually failed to overcome. The officer stated, 'You are strangers here, and do not understand the people or their problems. You build schools where market places are needed and vice versa, with no regard for the needs or desires of the people.' The conclusion of a historian of the American civic action program could have applied equally to the Australian effort. Robert Wilensky in *Military Medicine to Win Hearts and Minds* noted that civic action benefited individuals but not the government.

The SAS

While 1 ATF's infantry battalion's main focus was on large operations, the masters of the small engagement were the soldiers of the Special Air Service Regiment (SAS). While some SAS troopers had deployed to Vietnam with the AATTV in 1962 it was not until 1966 that a complete unit arrived and joined 1 ATF in the battle against the Viet Cong in Phuoc Tuy. The main reason for this late presence was simple, the existing SAS structure was already fully involved in the Confrontation with Indonesia in Borneo and the Regiment had to expand before there was sufficient personnel to support two conflicts. All three SAS Squadrons would serve in Vietnam, each more than once.

In early March 1966 Prime Minister Harold Holt revealed that 3 Squadron SAS would join 1 ATF as part of Australia's enlarged commitment to the Vietnam War. At that time 3 Squadron was still in the process of forming up and it was not entirely clear that it would finish its training by the time it was due to depart in late June. Complicating the matter further was that the Army did not have a clear idea on how 1 ATF should task the SAS. There was some concern within the Regiment that the Squadron would be used to supplement the formation's stretched infantry, or even be broken up into packets to assist the battalions. If this proved the case then 3 Squadron would have to retrain itself for an entirely different role once it arrived in theatre.

SAS soldiers en route to a patrol zone. Shown are Trooper John Pile and Sergeant John Gebhardt.
AWM FAI/70/0305/VN.

However, when 3 Squadron reached Nui Dat it became clear that the COMATF, Brigadier Jackson, understood the value of having the SAS as a part of his organisation. Jackson saw the SAS as his eyes and ears. The SAS were to provide the Task Force with intelligence on the enemy's organisation, whereabouts and movements. In Phuoc Tuy, the most reliable method to obtain this information was with small patrols, the ideal mission for the SAS and one with which they were familiar from their experiences in Borneo.

The typical SAS patrol consisted of either five or six men, although many contained just four. Army Headquarters had wanted the patrols to contain no less than ten soldiers, but after trials the lower number received approval. A patrol entered its area of operations on foot, perhaps after being dropped off nearby by either the Task Force's APCs or a helicopter of 9 Squadron, RAAF. The SAS would develop particularly close relationships with the RAAF's chopper crews.

Patrolling was lonely and arduous work, but it was also the only way to get Australian eyes into the enemy's base areas. The experiences of Lieutenant P. J. Schuman would have been typical. Leading a four man patrol, Schuman cautiously moved through a mix of bamboo, scrub and timber about two kilometres east of Long Tan. Every ten minutes he and his men stopped and listened for several minutes. The first sign of the enemy's presence was an increase in the number of flies. This either signified a dead animal or a camp latrine. With another member of the patrol, Schuman crawled slowly ahead, leaving the others in a cover position. After about 15 minutes they could hear voices and saw some huts. Unfortunately, at about the same time, a sentry spotted them, too. Schuman fired first, killing the VC, while the rest of the patrol opened up and advanced on the huts. As the Australians reached the VC's base the enemy broke and fled. The Australians gathered up the documents and equipment they found and moved to an extraction point to await the helicopter that Schuman had requested. The results might appear negligible– one VC dead and some items captured – but a successful intelligence picture is built slowly, piece by piece, in small increments.

Sometimes a patrol found itself too successful: it located far too many VC and placed itself in a precarious position. Second Lieutenant Bill Hindson was in command of a patrol near Thua Tich in the province's North-East. Helicopters had brought them in at tree height level and, almost as soon as they set down, there was evidence that the enemy was nearby. The next day they spotted four VC, and later in the day as the Australians filled their water bottles, they listened to the enemy fill their own around a bend in the creek. On day two, while observing from some dense undergrowth, the patrol spotted another VC about 15 metres away. Progressively, more enemy appeared until Hindson had counted 63 pass by – there were just five Australians in total. Later in the day, the patrol moved out and as they crossed a track a VC emerged nearby. A fire fight quickly developed as the patrol withdrew. Hindson called in a helicopter and the patrol escaped with one wounded. Within forty-five minutes of the contact the Australians were aloft and an air strike had bombed the enemy's position.

An SAS patrol arrives back at Nui Dat. Shown are Lance Corporal George Mach, Sergeant John O'Keefe and Trooper Dave Crompton (left to right).
AWM FAI/70/0313/VN.

In 1967 the COMAFV, Major General Tim Vincent, identified the SAS as the Task Force's most effective killers. The infantry were usually only successful in bringing the VC to battle when the enemy chose to make a stand, such as they had done at Long Tan and Binh Ba. However, SAS ambushes often resulted in one or two enemy killed, and while not dramatic successes, each encounter contributed to the VC's attrition and helped to reduce the enemy's morale, while also providing the Task Force with critical intelligence. The SAS also denied the VC the security of their base areas, because Australia's 'silent killers' could be almost anywhere in the province. It is not surprising that one of the rumours that circulated Phuoc Tuy was that the VC had placed a bounty on every SAS trooper's head – dead or alive.

Benefits and Costs Compared

Search and destroy and cordon and search operations lay at the core of the American and Australian method of waging war in Vietnam. The American Army's mission preference was obvious: search and destroy was the heart and soul of the institution's concept and was the basis of Westmoreland's strategy of attrition. For the Australians the choice between search and destroy and cordon and search was less clear than it was for the Americans. The Australian doctrine of counter-insurgency warfare identified as its priorities the separation of the insurgents from the villages, and the winning of the indigenous population's hearts and minds. While search and destroy had a role in pushing the enemy's main force units away from the villages, cordon and search struck more directly at the enemy's vital ground—the communists' village structure and the cadres.

In Vietnam, 1 ATF operated under American command in an American-dominated battlespace. Search and destroy operations, therefore, were a fact of life for the task force. In fact, some ATF Commanders embraced the destruction of the VC main force units as wholeheartedly as did the Americans, and made it the focus of the task force's operations.

Australian interest in cordon and search as an operational methodology was strongest during the deployment's first years under Jackson, and especially under Graham. Under Hughes, the next ATF Commander, 1 ATF spent much of its time outside Phuoc Tuy assisting the Americans in countering the VC in the two Tet Offensives. However, after Hughes, Australian commanders leaned decidedly towards killing the VC in battle. When Pearson took command in September 1969 he accepted that his options were either to operate against the VC main force units or focus on pacification measures. Pearson rightly knew he did not have the strength to do both, and decided to destroy one of the task force's oldest nemeses: the VC *275 Regiment*. The following May, a month before the end of his tour, he admitted that the task force was still chasing the enemy's units, and pacification continued to languish in importance. Next in command was Weir. He believed that the task force 'had the job of hammering away at the enemy Main Force, and the enemy Local Force formed units, which were in fact 'big brother' to all the little guerrilla units that existed at every village and hamlet.' What Weir appears to have overlooked was that not only had the enemy's main force units survived annihilation, despite years of concerted effort on the part of the task force, but that the VC also still controlled the villages. The last ATF Commander was Brigadier B. A. McDonald. He too saw his role as bringing the VC's forces to battle.

The efforts to kill the VC main force units were not without effect. During Brigadier W. G. Henderson's time with 1 ATF (June 1970–Februay 1971) the VC main force had a much reduced presence in Phuoc Tuy. The enemy even broke up *D440 Battalion* in order to reinforce its other units. Henderson credits Pearson's aggressiveness with having forced the VC to move elsewhere. However what was not so readily recognised was that moving the VC over the border was not the equivalent of destroying the enemy. The task force simply made Phuoc Tuy's VC into someone else's problem, and when the pressure relaxed the enemy's main force units slipped back into the province.

The 5 RAR historian, Robert O'Neill, compared the effectiveness of the battalion's search and destroy missions with its cordon and search operations. In 1966, 5 RAR conducted eight search and destroy missions and five cordon and search operations. The Australian and VC casualties were:

- search and destroy:
  Australian - 6 KIA, 31 WIA
  VC – 33 KIA, 2 POW
- cordon and search:
  Australian – 1 KIA, 0 WIA
  VC – 16 KIA, 47 POW, 112 suspects identified

While the sample set from which these figures was drawn is small, the figures do suggest that cordon and search operations were the more effective means by which to weaken the VC. While 5 RAR undertook only five cordon and search operations they accounted for more VC than the battalion's eight search and destroy missions. Also of note was that the battalion suffered negligible casualties from cordon and search operations.

Radio communication was essential to coordinate movement through Phuoc Tuy's rugged terrain. Here Corporal Felix Byrne of 1 RAR keeps contact with a platoon during Operation *Hawkesbury*.
AWM ERR/68/0897/VN.

However there were limiting factors on the Australian ability to undertake cordon and search operations, namely:

- the requirement for high-quality local intelligence in order to distinguish between active insurgents, VC sympathisers, and ordinary villagers; and
- the requirement for close cooperation with provincial officials because the protection of the villages was the GVN's TAOR.

In addition, unlike in Malaya, the VC main force units were a real threat and had to be contained.

These requirements were difficult to fulfil in Phuoc Tuy. Until far too late in the war, liaison remained limited between the task force and provincial GVN officials. In addition, intelligence collection and analysis suffered from an oversupply of agencies and lacked a joint approach. Lastly, the three allied forces operating in Phuoc Tuy never developed a joint war vision nor command structure.

Yet, in the face of generally poor results, search and destroy missions did offer one benefit to the allies. By seeking out the enemy's main force units the Americans and Australians kept their opponent on the move which, in turn, limited the VC's ability to initiate their own plans. However, it must be recognised that confounding enemy operations was an unintended benefit, and shifting the VC from one AO to another only prolonged the campaign which, in the long run, favoured the communists' concept of war.

Even as the Australian deployment neared its end, 1 ATF continued to perform search and destroy operations. However, despite six years of experience in such missions the results continued to disappoint. In June 1971 the Australians launched Operation *Overlord*. With American assistance the forces involved amounted to almost the equivalent of a division in strength. 4 RAR's unit history summarised the operation's results: Own – 1 WIA, VC – 1 KIA. *Overlord* suggests that the Australians, like the Americans, suffered from two intellectual failures. The two forces had been unable to develop an effective method to 'find, fix and finish' the VC, and in the face of failure, both armies lacked the honesty to appropriately examine their methods, the determination to seek out tactical improvements, and the strength of will to implement new practices. More importantly, the Australians had forgotten one of the key lessons of their experiences in Malaya—it was the cadres in the villages that really mattered.

Lesson 18

In a multi-national environment, joint command is essential if operations are to be integrated into a single war effort. Without coordination and cooperation allied strength will dissipate and operations will be less effective and efficient.

Lesson 19

If plans do not deliver the desired results it is essential to have the intellectual honesty to admit failure and the strength of will to develop and implement new methods. Failure will continue—unless the enemy makes even greater mistakes of their own. It is unwise to rely on enemy incompetence to achieve success.

URBAN OPERATIONS

Urban Warfare and the Vietnam War

Commonly held images of combat in Phuoc Tuy are that of a patrol stealthily moving through the jungle, a group of soldiers patiently waiting in ambush, or a body of troops silhouetted against a rice paddy. It is comparatively rare to see images of Australians fighting in the urban environment. However, in contrast to the stereotype, some of the bitterest fighting of the Vietnam War took place in the country's cities. The biggest, lengthiest, and most brutal example of urban warfare was the struggle for Hue during the Tet Offensive of February 1968, a contest which ended in the VC's defeat and the city's destruction.

Tet was a relatively minor affair in Phuoc Tuy when compared to the fighting that took place in the other regions of Vietnam, and most of the task force was out of the province when the storm struck. In Phuoc Tuy the VC limited their efforts to the province's capital of Ba Ria, which they occupied before dawn on 1 February. 1 ATF responded by dispatching its ready reaction force from Nui Dat to assist the city's defenders. After a 24-hour struggle the Australians drove the enemy from the city.

The defining conditions of urban warfare are: a closed-in environment, limited and short-range line of sight, point-blank engagement, intensive use of firepower, and widespread availability of easily fortified defensive positions. To successfully counter the defender's advantages the attacker must rely on small unit assaults supported by heavy firepower and combined arms tactics.

The definition of urban warfare as described above also applied equally to another Vietnam environment, however. The VC typically hid their bases under the jungle canopy where the insurgents were safe from observation from the air. To defend these bases from ground assault the communists dug deep, constructing networks of bunkers, communication trenches and tunnels. The communists laid out their positions so as to be mutually supporting, thereby providing their garrisons with interlocking lanes of fire over the pre-designated killing ground. Access was typically through a tunnel or trench, and the VC often connected their bunkers into sets with trench-like passageways which the enemy used to shift between fire positions, a tactic that also had the effect of magnifying the communists' strength.

A bunker's only exposed part was its small fire slit. Most of the structure was below ground level, and the VC blended the bunker's opening so skilfully into the surrounding foliage that it was virtually invisible, at least while its occupants held their fire. Roofed with layers of logs and dirt it was also impervious to anything but a direct hit from a large shell or bomb.

There were in actuality two urban-type environments in Phuoc Tuy. Battles in the province's towns and villages were relatively rare and there are only a handful of examples. By contrast, bunker battles were extremely common. Every 1 ATF patrol that ventured into the jungle did so with the knowledge that the Australians might encounter a VC bunker system. When this happened the Australians found themselves fighting in conditions that mimicked those of street fighting: point-blank range, heavily fortified defence, limited line of sight, and the need for firepower to crack open the enemy's positions.

The Battle for Binh Ba

The most determined and bloody urban-style battle that 1 ATF fought took place in the village of Binh Ba from 6 to 8 June 1969. It was the VC who initiated the contact, perhaps the only instance of the insurgents directly challenging the Australians in Phuoc Tuy since their defeat at Long Tan in 1966. The VC's determination for battle proved a costly mistake. The Australians took advantage of the enemy's willingness to stand and fight, brought the task force's firepower to bear, and made the VC pay a heavy price.

The village of Binh Ba lay in the Duc Thanh District just west of Route 2 and about five kilometres north of the Australian base at Nui Dat. It was a large village of over two thousand people, many of whom worked in the adjacent Gallia Rubber Plantation. The village contained nearly 200 sturdy houses made of brick and concrete and red tiled roofs, laid out in a neat grid. The task force had previous experience in Binh Ba. In 1966, 5 RAR undertook Operation *Holsworthy*, a cordon and search mission of Binh Ba and its satellite hamlets of Duc Trung and Duc My. Although this was a success—5 RAR rounded up a large number of insurgents and sympathisers—the task force was never able to sever the VC's influence over the population.

It is not known why the VC decided to fight for Binh Ba. Pearson, the 1 ATF Commander at the time, later speculated that the enemy had infiltrated Binh Ba in order to ambush an Australian supply column. A second explanation is more complex and suggests that the Australians provoked the VC into seeking the confrontation because of the task force's actions elsewhere. On 31 May, 6 RAR/NZ (ANZAC) commenced Operation *Lavarack*, a search and destroy mission whose AO was to the north-west of Binh Ba. *Lavarack*'s target was the *33 NVA Regiment*, known to be operating in the area. The VC may have entered Binh Ba to divert the task force's attention and thereby relieve the pressure on *33 NVA Regiment*.

Brigadier C. M. I. Pearson, 1 ATF Commander, 1968–1969.
AWM BEL/69/0433/VN.

The two sides made contact at 0810 hours when an insurgent fired a RPG7 from a village building at a passing Australian tank and armoured recovery vehicle. The round struck the tank, penetrated the armour and wounded one of the crew who lay slumped across the main gun. The tank's commander, Lance Corporal John Harvey, responded by strafing the house from which the VC had fired the rocket with .30 calibre machine-gun fire, while the recovery vehicle also opened up with its own machine-guns. Harvey then continued on to the Regional Force Post in Duc Thanh to evacuate his wounded crewman and to alert the garrison of the VC's presence in Binh Ba. The recovery vehicle returned to Nui Dat.

Two Regional Force Platoons moved out of Duc Thanh to investigate the situation in Binh Ba. As they approached the village, the VC stopped them with heavy RPG and automatic weapon fire. At this point the district chief requested support from provincial headquarters in Ba Ria, which, in turn, sought 1 ATF's assistance. At 0900 hours, just 50 minutes after the first contact, the ready reaction force at Nui Dat went on alert.

APCs, Centurion tanks and infantry of 5 RAR engage VC in the rubber plantation outside Binh Ba.
AWM BEL/69/0382/VN.

On 6 June the units tasked as the ready reaction force were D Company 5 RAR, a composite troop of four Centurion tanks drawn from B Squadron 1 Armoured Regiment, and 3 Troop B Squadron 3 Cavalry Regiment. The on-call battery was 105 Field Battery. At 0900 hours, officers attended a hastily assembled briefing at Nui Dat. The ready reaction team lived up to its name and by 1030 hours it had concentrated just south of Binh Ba. The mission received the designation Operation *Hammer*, and its senior officer was the D Company Commander, Major Murray Blake.

As the Australians headed north to relieve Binh Ba they anticipated meeting only light resistance. The intelligence assessment they had received concluded that the VC had at most one or two platoons in the village. This proved a gross underestimation. Intelligence officers had little more than guesses from which to make their deductions but one fact was clear: since the Battle of Long Tan the enemy's main force units had shown little inclination to initiate a battle in Phuoc Tuy.

While the relief task group had no way knowing in advance that today was the day that the VC had decided to make a stand and fight, the enemy did offer some hints of the change in their tactical attitude. As the column drove past Duc My, it came under automatic weapon fire, which the tanks paused to silence. The VC attacked again, this time with RPGs, when the relief force reached a clearing just south of Binh Ba and its tanks and APCs deployed off the road. In response, the tanks levelled the houses from which the fire had come. The two instances suggested an unusually aggressive opponent who was confident enough to take on tanks, and who occupied a larger area than was possible for a force of one or two platoons as the intelligence report suggested. In fact, the VC force in Binh Ba was *1 Battalion, 33 NVA Regiment* supported by the *Binh Ba Guerrilla Platoon*, and possibly other local units. At least a company of VC infantry and the battalion headquarters were in Binh Ba itself, with the rest of the unit under cover nearby.

The Australians paused before commencing their assault on Binh Ba to allow the district chief to ascertain whether the villagers had evacuated. Since built-up areas were the provincial government's TAOR, it was up to the district chief to give the Australians clearance to engage the enemy. In authorising the assault the district chief told the Australians, 'It is as clear as we can make it. Go in and do what you have to do.' However, once the battle began villagers continued to make their way out of the fighting, a process with which the VC did not interfere. Some families even spent the entire battle in the basements of their homes, not emerging until after the conflagration above them had passed by.

> **Lesson 20**
>
> Intelligence reports are almost always indicative not absolute. Commanders must reconsider the assessment of their opponent's strength, situation and bearing as new information becomes available. If the enemy adopts an aggressive posture it may indicate greater strength than intelligence assessments initially suggested.

At 1120 hours the Australians entered Binh Ba from the east. The tanks led down parallel streets with a section of APCs supporting each of the flank Centurions. Behind the centre tanks came the APC Troop headquarters element. Bringing up the rear was a third APC section. D Company began the action mounted in the APCs, although 11 Platoon soon dismounted from the rear section to help shepherd civilians from the danger zone.

The tanks advanced methodically in short bounds using the village's buildings for protection from the enemy's RPGs. At first, resistance was light, but as the Australians neared Binh Ba's centre the amount of incoming firepower increased significantly, and it seemed to the Australians that they faced considerably more than one or two platoons of VC. Blake spotted a VC team towing a wheeled heavy machine-gun, which suggested to him that the enemy had brought up a heavy weapon company.

As the tanks advanced, word came through the radio net from an observation aircraft that an enemy group of approximately company size was moving through the rubber. The two right-hand tanks immediately left the village, drove to its western side and engaged the VC. In the process of leaving Binh Ba one of the tanks was hit by an RPG7 which penetrated the turret, wounding three of the crew. Unable to traverse the turret, the gunner continued to fire HE and canister at the VC whenever they crossed his line of sight.

Two Australian M113A1 APCs. Towards the end of 1966, 1 ATF upgraded some of its APCs, adding enclosed turrets. The turret mounted either twin L3A3 Browning .30 cal machine-guns or one M2HB .50 cal Browning and one L3A3 .30 cal Browning machine-gun.
Mark Wahlert.

M113A1 Armoured Personnel Carrier (USA)

Length: 4.86 m
Width: 2.69 m
Height:
1.85 m (to top of hull)
Weight: 11,515 kg
Crew:
commander & driver
Power plant:
GM 215 hp 6-cyl diesel (M113A1)
Armament:
1 x .50-in MG, or twin .30-in MGs, or a .50 & .30 MG combination
Max Armour: 45 mm
Speed: 68 kph

The M113 APC first appeared in 1960. It was designed to transport a squad of 11 infantrymen while providing them with protection from small arms fire. Made from aluminium alloy, the M113 was light enough to be air-transportable, air-droppable and swimmable. However, it was vulnerable to mines, RPGs and armour-piercing rounds. It was a versatile and reliable vehicle that became a common sight in Vietnam and was used extensively by both US and Australian forces. Variants used by the Australian Army in Vietnam included M113A1 (FS) Fire Support Vehicle [with 76 mm gun]; M125A1 Armoured Mortar Carrier; M577A1 Armoured Command Vehicle; and M113A1 (F) Armoured Fitters Vehicle.

Centurion Tanks of B Squadron 1 Armoured Regiment manoeuvre on a road. AWM WAR/70/0056/VN.

Centurion Mk5/1MBT (UK)

Crew:
    4, commander, driver,
    gunner, loader
Weight: 50,802 kg
Length: 9.75 m (overall)
Width: 3.4 m
Height: 2.98 m
Power plant:
    Rolls Royce Meteor 12
    cylinder petrol engine
Speed: 34.6 kph
Armament:
    20-pdr main gun; .50-in
    Browning M2 ranging
    MG; two .30-in Browning
    M1919A4 MGs; 12 smoke
    dischargers
Max Armour: 152 mm

The British Centurion Mk3 main battle tank was the mainstay of the British Army in the post-Second World War period. It was purchased by the Australian Army in 1951 and served in Vietnam with 1 Armoured Regt from 1968 until 1971. The original Mk3 Centurions in the Australian Army were all upgraded to Mk5/1 in time for service in Vietnam. While its deployment to Vietnam had many sceptics, the Centurion soon proved its effectiveness, just as the Matilda tank had done in supporting Australian infantry in the jungles of the South-West Pacific against the Japanese. In particular, the Centurion proved vital in the provision of mobile fire support and in a bunker-busting role. The Centurion's armour was not invulnerable, however, and the VC could penetrate it with the RPG7.

When the right flank tank commanders opted to leave the rest of the task group in order to attack the manoeuvring VC they did so on their own initiative. Neither the group's overall commander, Blake, nor the tank troop commander, Lieutenant Brian Sullivan, had authorised the manoeuvre or even knew of it. As the tanks left they also broke contact with their supporting APCs who remained behind. While poor formation discipline, opportunism, and lack of a clear chain of command were the main factors in the tanks' disappearance, the inability of the three teams making up the task group to communicate among themselves was significant. While Blake remained mounted, the APC troop commander, Captain Ray De Vere, was in command of the task group. However the noise of the battle was so great and radio communication so difficult that no one was effectively

> **Lesson 21**
>
> Imprecise, unclear and shifting divisions of command impede the effective control of battle. Command authority derives from the combination of mission assets, requirements and objectives, not, for example, from variable changes in means of transport. The management of battle requires clear command authority that must be in place before combat commences.

in charge. In addition, the infantry could not communicate directly with any of the tanks because their external phones were either broken or missing. At one point in the battle the infantry discovered the best way to get the crew's attention was to shoot a burst of automatic weapon fire at the tank's side.

Although the tanks that left Binh Ba inflicted heavy casualties on the VC they intercepted, their action effectively halved the number of Centurions available to the task group just as the Australians approached the enemy's main zone of defence. The task group would miss the tanks' presence. When the two remaining tanks reached the middle of the village they became the centre of the VC's attention. The air was thick with RPG missiles, and for two hours the VC maintained steady and heavy pressure on the Australians. Blake described the intensity of the noise as 'horrendous'. The tanks replied with canister, firing at clusters of VC as they darted around the village or blasted the enemy from houses that they had converted into bastions. The tanks discovered that if they fired a HE (high explosive) round at a house's wooden door instead of trying to shoot through a building's wall, the round blew down the door and exploded inside the house. The house's wall contained the blast and the structure suffered less damage, while the shock wave killed the insurgents inside. No further enemy fire came from houses treated with this technique.

At about 1300 hours Blake decided that it was time to leave. The tanks were running out of ammunition, whereas it appeared as if the VC had limitless numbers of RPGs. Blake accepted that the task group had driven into the midst of a major VC force and that the Australians were at risk of envelopment and destruction. Casualties were not high, but only because the VC focused their fury on the tanks, not the more vulnerable APCs. If the VC succeeded in knocking out the tanks, or if the tanks ran out of ammunition, it would be the turn of the APCs and the infantry to bear the brunt of the enemy's attack.

Blake directed the task group southwards in order to break out of the village and reach open ground. To convey his intention to De Vere he literally had to grab the APC commander by the throat, because the noise was so great. Radio communication was impossible. As the task group neared the exit, the VC stopped them with a steady barrage of RPG rounds that emanated from the last two rows of houses. Fortunately, Sullivan was able to access the FAC net and obtain assistance from the US air controller. Two RAAF helicopter gunships also responded and fired their rockets into the houses. Enemy insurgents poured from these buildings and the task group opened fire on them and the buildings into which they fled. At this point the tanks pushed past the final line of buildings, and with the APCs close behind, into the open.

All of the tanks had been damaged, one so severely that it was withdrawn, and all had used up much of their ammunition. Sullivan's tank had exhausted its HE and he broke out of Binh Ba with the last round of canister loaded. But by this time reinforcements had arrived. B Company 5 RAR had come up from Nui Dat and the CO of the battalion, Lieutenant-Colonel Colin Khan, had arrived to take command. Khan also brought with him his AT (anti-tank) platoon. A fresh troop of tanks had arrived, driving south from where they had been supporting 6 RAR/NZ (ANZAC) on Operation *Lavarack*.

Lesson 23

If different arms are to wage effective combined arms warfare they must be equipped for seamless communication. It should not be easier for a FO or FAC to bring to bear distant assets than for an infantry officer to communicate with an adjacent tank. Any failure to integrate communications between the arms sharing the same battlespace is senseless.

At 1400 hours the Australians entered Binh Ba again, this time sweeping from the west to the east. They made contact almost at once, and battle was again joined. Murray now had clear command and in this sweep he maintained close control over the task group. D Company entered Binh Ba dismounted and led the way with the infantry and armour working together as a team. When the foot soldiers spotted the enemy they pinned them with small arms fire. This protected the tanks from the enemy's RPGs and allowed the armour to come forward. The tanks blew a hole in the house in which the VC sheltered and then followed up with a round of canister fired through the gap. As this happened, the APCs put down suppressive fire with their machine-guns, allowing the infantry to close on the target. Once in place, the infantry tossed grenades into the building and, after their detonation, charged inside to clear the house room by room, finishing off any remaining VC in a hand-to-hand struggle. Street by street, building by building, room by room, the task group made its way across the village. By dusk the job was still not done and the Australians moved into a night defensive leaguer.

At 0600 hours on 7 June the battle resumed. B Company 5 RAR encountered a company-strength force of VC moving through the rubber on the south-west corner of Binh Ba. A firefight developed that also involved tanks and APCs before the VC broke contact. At 0950 hours 5 RAR began another sweep on Binh Ba with armour and sapper support. It soon became clear that most of the VC had slipped away in the night, although they did take a few wounded VC prisoner. At 1300 hours the battle flared anew when the VC attacked the nearby Regional Force Post in Duc Trung. On the morning of 8 June, 5 RAR undertook a final sweep of Binh Ba and then handed over to 1 Civil Affairs Unit which arrived to help with the resettlement of those villagers whose homes had been destroyed. Operation *Hammer* was officially over.

If the enemy's intention had been to relieve the pressure that 6 RAR/NZ (ANZAC) had applied to *33 NVA Regiment* during Operation *Lavarack*, then the plan failed. Operation *Lavarack* continued without respite. The enemy's boldness came at a heavy price; they suffered more than 100 KIA.

The aftermath of the battle for Binh Ba. The Australians have laid out the VC dead in the central square to check for documents before burial.
AWM BEL/69/0388/VN.

Bunker Busting

Within Phuoc Tuy's jungle and mountainous areas the communists had built numerous base camps for their main and regional force units. Invariably they protected these installations with bunker systems. 1 ATF in its operations to find and destroy the VC had to patrol into the areas in which the enemy had their refuges. When they happened, contacts invariably involved an Australian assault on an enemy's bunker system.

Bunker systems varied in size depending on the installations they protected. Thus a VC platoon camp might have only a handful of bunkers, while a larger facility might number in the hundreds. One particularly big find occurred during Operation *Camden*. 5 RAR uncovered the headquarters of VC Military Region 5 whose complex contained approximately 2000 bunkers. The one constant was that the Australians had little knowledge of a bunker system's scale, or even its existence, until they found it. In addition, combat was often initiated by the VC who held their fire until the Australians had entered the killing zone. In most bunker encounters the Australians suffered the majority of their losses in the contact's opening seconds.

A soldier from 9 RAR aims his rifle into a bunker during Operation *Goodwood*. AWM EKN/69/0023/VN.

The Australians developed two basic techniques for dealing with a bunker system. The patrol either followed up its discovery with an immediate assault or disengaged temporarily in order to bring up reinforcements, coordinate fire support to soften up the target, and organise a set-piece attack before re-entering the enemy's camp.

The CO of 5 RAR, Khan, outlined the pros and cons of both techniques. He believed that immediate assault was only feasible when attacking a small bunker system that was guarded by a small number of VC. In an immediate assault the idea was to force the communists to flee so that the Australians captured the camp intact, which was important for intelligence collecting. Also, by attacking immediately, the Australians struck before the VC had time to organise their defence.

Since under the immediate assault model the Australians attacked without the opportunity to assess the enemy's strength and bearing, the action had the potential to lead to high casualties. In their aggressiveness, the Australians accepted the possibility that the enemy would be of superior strength. Under the immediate assault model, supporting fire would also be of limited assistance. While artillery and aircraft fire could isolate the battlefield and interdict the enemy's retreat route, they could not safely fire into the bunker system while the infantry attempted a quick advance. Once committed, the infantry had to succeed on its own. If the VC were present in numbers, the Australians' only recourse was to disengage and switch to more deliberate methods.

Khan's preference was to have the troops who made the initial contact pull back to allow the battalion the opportunity to develop a methodical attack which would bring to bear 1 ATF's and II FFV's firepower. When a 5 RAR patrol made contact with a VC bunker system, Khan flew to the scene in a helicopter to coordinate the battle from the air. From his high observation point over the VCs position, Khan had a better sense of the battlespace than his platoon and company commanders could achieve on the ground. Hovering above, Khan could also marshal Australian and American fire support, and integrate it into the developing battle below. While the FO with the troops in contact remained responsible for bringing the guns into play, Khan controlled the battalion radio net and was in position to halt fire so that helicopter gunships and fixed wing aircraft could launch strikes. Only once the support arms had sufficiently worked over the target did he allow the infantry to advance again into the bunker system.

A Centurion Tank of C Squadron 1 Armoured Regiment pushes through the jungle on
Operation *Overlord* in June 1971.
AWM FOD/71/0305/VN.

Infantry from C Company 9 RAR patrol in front of a Centurion Tank during Operation *Surfside* in 1969.
AWM COM/69/0250/VN.

1 Armoured Regiment's addition to the task force in 1968 complemented rather than changed the task force's bunker-clearing practices. Despite its great bulk the Centurion tank manoeuvred well in the confined space of the jungle, pushing over trees to open pathways and firing canister to clear lines of sight through the dense foliage. In the jungle, as in an urban setting, it was essential for the infantry and armour to work together, each protecting and supporting the other.

While on Operation *Iron Fox*, a search and destroy mission in Phuoc Tuy's north, 4 RAR/NZ (ANZAC) discovered a major base complex that belonged to VC *274 Regiment*. On 30 July alone the battalion destroyed over 200 bunkers. However the next morning, after D Company moved just 200 yards from its night harbour, the Australians found an even larger VC bunker complex. As the infantry pressed forward to ascertain the size of this new complex the call went out for tank support.

'Bunker Buster'. 1 Armoured Regiment's Centurion tanks proved critical in the destruction of enemy bunkers. In this scene the tank fires at a virtually invisible VC bunker. Australian infantry are nearby, protecting the tank and also locating more targets. Gouache on board.
Jeff Isaacs, OAM.

When the Centurions arrived after scrub bashing their way through the jungle, they found the infantry already engaged against a numerous and well-armed opponent. For the infantry the main problems were avoiding being crushed by the tanks and the falling trees that they pushed over, and communication with their mates inside the armoured vehicles. The two arms did not share a radio net and the phone mounted on the Centurion's rear—if it had not been knocked off—was positioned so that its use required an infantryman to expose himself to enemy fire. For the tanks the difficulties lay in target acquisition and avoiding the enemy's RPG7s. For the foot soldiers there was an additional danger. They had to make sure never to be forward of the tank's second road wheel when it fired its main armament: the blast wave could be deadly.

The tanks depended on the infantry to find them targets and to suppress the VC's rocket teams. The infantry needed the armour to destroy the enemy's bunkers so that they could advance. APCs also stood by to bring up more ammunition and to withdraw the wounded. The arms took a painstaking approach to the reduction of the bunker system. When the infantry identified a target, the tank destroyed it with a HE round. At times, due to the thickness of the foliage, the tank crew had to aim by sighting down the barrel. If the bunker could not be hit with gunfire the tank simply drove on top and executed a quick track turn, collapsing the structure and entombing the defenders. If the enemy attempted to run, the tank fired an anti-personnel canister round and the VC disappeared.

The introduction of tanks to Vietnam was not without controversy, and there had been some reluctance to deploy them. However, as they had in New Guinea in the Second World War, tanks again proved themselves as effective jungle fighters. The availability of powerful, mobile and direct firepower saved infantry lives when they otherwise would have had to rely on their M72s or close assault to clear VC bunkers. When the Australian government returned 1 Armoured Regiment to Australia as part of the withdrawal from Vietnam, the task of the infantry remaining in Phuoc Tuy became harder and more dangerous.

The penultimate ATF Commander, Henderson, assessed the place of the tank in his post-tour interview. He concluded:

> I believe if any force is deployed anywhere in the world again by Australia and they go without tanks, we need our heads read. Most useful, a lifesaver in situations such as a bunker situation ... they are the only thing to use if we are going to save that infantryman ...

THE INTELLIGENCE WAR

Intelligence in Phuoc Tuy

Based on its experiences in Malaya and Borneo, the Australian Army accepted that the key to victory in a counter-insurgency-style conflict was access to timely, reliable and high-quality intelligence of operational value. In discussing the lessons of his command of 1 ATF, Jackson extended the army's doctrinal observations on the importance of intelligence to include the war in Vietnam. He observed, 'I think our greatest single problem in counter-insurgency warfare operations is the collection and collation of intelligence. I am sure this is more important than it has ever been to any army before.'

Sapper Barry Hartford crawls through a VC tunnel during Operation *Enoggera*. Often the best intelligence was the information that the task force collected itself.
AWM CUN/66/0523/VN.

There was a direct correlation between the availability of intelligence and the success of the task force's campaign in Phuoc Tuy. When asked his opinion on how to measure whether military operations were leading towards victory, Australia's counter-insurgency expert, Colonel Ted Serong, identified intelligence as his indicator. Serong took exception to the American practice of gauging success as a statistical function derived from the analysis of data such as the enemy's body count, the number of allied missions launched, or the tonnage of ordnance expended by batteries and squadrons. Instead, he preferred an intangible measurement. Serong insisted that the best indicator of progress in a counter-insurgency conflict was the growing willingness of the people to offer spontaneous high-quality intelligence.

The types of intelligence the task force required were not dissimilar to those which a combatant needs in a conventional war. The two main elements of these types of intelligence are knowledge of the operational environment and the enemy. The combatant must understand the enemy's command and force structure, their method of operations, their weaponry, their state of training, their vulnerabilities and their logistics. In addition, in a counter-insurgency conflict, a detailed understanding of the enemy's infrastructure—in particular its local organisation, identity of cadres, committee members and sympathisers, and methods of coordination and contact with the field forces—is also vital.

While the task force accomplished much during its time in Phuoc Tuy, it never gained a decisive and exploitable advantage over the VC through its intelligence efforts. In fact, intelligence shortfalls proved an intractable problem for the Australians. There were numerous explanations for this failure, but the main reasons lay in a lack of unity of effort in Phuoc Tuy, inadequate intelligence staffing levels at Nui Dat, and a task force wide deficiency in knowledge of Vietnamese language and culture.

The poor intelligence picture which planners faced at Nui Dat was not a result of the unavailability of either raw information or resident intelligence agencies in the province. During Henderson's time Phuoc Tuy had between 12 and 14 active intelligence organisations. However, despite this number—or perhaps because of it—his successor, McDonald, observed that he 'never got a fair intel assessment throughout his tour from the myriad province orgs.'

Since there were too many independent intelligence agencies operating in the province, the volume of information flowing into intelligence centres often overwhelmed analysts. The multitude of agencies included desks for the GVN, ARVN, MACV and CIA, as well as representatives of each of the United States military services. In addition, the province was a seller's market; freelance agents peddled information to the highest bidder. Despite being the main military force in the province, the Australians had no control or oversight over any of these bodies. In fact, amongst these giants, 1 ATF's intelligence presence was comparatively minor.

Unfortunately, in Phuoc Tuy's fragmented intelligence environment, there was, for most of the war, no coordinating authority to make sense of the various sources, judge the value of the information, prioritise and analyse the material, or present it to field commanders in a timely manner. Moreover, information did not travel horizontally amongst the allied military representatives in the province. Each intelligence agency in Phuoc Tuy was an office of a larger organisation whose main presence was elsewhere. Consequently, information tended to move vertically as these myriad agencies reported up their chains of command. As a result, as soon as the information left the province, it was lost to the Australians.

It was not until 1970 that Phuoc Tuy's intelligence principals established a Joint Intelligence Committee. The committee met daily but, in the limited time remaining before 1 ATF's withdrawal, it did not materially improve the flow of actionable or useful intelligence to Nui Dat.

From its arrival in Phuoc Tuy, 1 ATF struggled to access operationally important intelligence. In part, this was due to the lack of personnel skilled in the Vietnamese language and who understood local cultural markers. Prisoners of war (POWs), deserters and detainees represented critical intelligence sources whose information often demanded a rapid operational reaction. However, an ongoing shortage of bi-lingual interrogators meant that the task force was frequently unable to exploit the information these individuals might have possessed. Instead, what typically happened was that the Australians transferred the persons of interest they had collected to an allied processing centre. Once this happened, however, any information they held was lost to the Australian network.

Compounding the task force's language deficiencies was the relatively low staff level of intelligence corps members on Nui Dat's establishment. At the peak of its strength in South Vietnam, about 2 per cent of the United States' entire establishment was intelligence operators. A postwar report estimated that the figure for the South Vietnamese forces was between 6 and 7 per cent. By contrast, the number of Australian intelligence personnel in Vietnam represented approximately .05 per cent of the deployment's total strength—a figure which also included intelligence postings outside of Nui Dat.

The Australian task force made widespread use of field radios in Vietnam. Their presence pushed battlefield command and control down to platoon level. Infantry commanders had called for the allocation of radios to sections, but this step was not taken. The photo is of Private Peter O'Halloran, a signaller with C Company 2 RAR.
AWM FOD/71/0255/VN.

The reality was that the Australian Army had little option but to undersupply intelligence personnel posted to Vietnam. A .05 per cent of deployed strength translated into 20 per cent of the entire Australian Intelligence Corps establishment. From this perspective the Intelligence Corps was already doing all it could to help in Vietnam. A prerequisite, therefore, to raising the percentage of intelligence personnel serving in Vietnam was an expansion of the Australian Intelligence Corps, and its ongoing maintenance at a higher establishment. This, of course, would take time.

The number of intelligence personnel posted to Vietnam did increase gradually. In May 1966 the intelligence establishment was just 4 officers and 17 ORs, divided between HQ AFV, HQ 1 ATF, 1 Division Intelligence Unit, and HQ 1 ALSG. Although never numerous, the deployment's intelligence personnel reached a peak of 9 officers and 30 ORs, shared by the units listed above. While representing a near doubling of strength, the task force's intelligence establishment remained an understaffed resource. As a result, 1 ATF had severe problems in developing long-term intelligence assessments and lacked the manpower to develop a counter-insurgency database or to undertake research. Instead, the intelligence staff expended much of its energy sifting through the sea of materials that ebbed and flowed through the province in an effort to pick out the nuggets of immediate operational priority. A postwar assessment observed that the establishment of any future deployment should contain a much more robust intelligence establishment than was available to 1 ATF at Nui Dat.

Acorn Operations

The Australians did have one consistently successful operational intelligence achievement—the *Acorn* operation series. *Acorn* operations were similar to the cordon and search mission in that they sought to disrupt the enemy's village-level cadre and committee organisation. However, instead of the search of an entire village in the hope of discovering enemy agents and sympathisers who happened to be in residence, *Acorn* operations sought specific individuals whom intelligence staff had identified in advance. *Acorn* operations, in contrast to cordon and search missions, were less disruptive of the loyal population, and made more effective and efficient use of resources. According to Hughes, *Acorn* operations were the most successful type of mission undertaken by 1 ATF for striking at the enemy's village-level infrastructure.

1 ATF made widespread use of American heavy lift capability in Phuoc Tuy. Here a M2A2 howitzer is carried to an FSB slung below a CH-47 Chinook helicopter during Operation *Hawkesbury* in September 1968.
AWM P03872.001.

Acorn operations commenced in 1968 and continued up to the time of the Australian withdrawal, except for a lapse between September 1969 and September 1970. They were multi-national missions requiring cooperation between 1 ATF intelligence staffs and their opposites in the provincial administration. Participating in each mission were a mix of Australian soldiers and South Vietnamese military and police forces. The participants in *Acorn* 43, a raid of Dat Do on 24 May 1969, for example, were drawn from 1 ATF's 1 Division Intelligence Unit, 161 (Indep) Recce Flight and 3 SAS Squadron working with personnel from the Dat Do National Police. At most 1 ATF had to contribute the equivalent of a platoon of men and a couple of APCs to the typical *Acorn* operation, a commitment far smaller than that allocated for most other mission types. Consequently, *Acorn* operations brought good returns for a minimal investment in task force resources. Between 17 September and 27 November 1970, 1 ATF participated in 10 *Acorn* operations and netted 79 suspects. The haul included a number of confirmed VC, numerous suppliers, as well as suspects requiring further investigation by the provincial police. In addition, those participating in these raids discovered and destroyed several bunkers and recovered small quantities of weapons, ammunition and explosive devices. Also of importance was the fact that these operations involved minimal disruption to the lives of villagers who were loyal to the Saigon government.

In order to be effective, *Acorn* operations required the assembly, interpretation and coordination of local intelligence between 1 Division Intelligence Unit and Vietnamese intelligence agencies. These operations were dependent on the trust of the local people, as the initial source of information on suspects often came from someone else from the village. Due to the small scale of the operation, intelligence staffs moved quickly once they had confirmed a pattern of suspicious behaviour. Shortly thereafter a team of Australian soldiers and Vietnamese police swept into the village, surrounded the targeted houses, and captured the suspects. Often a team needed no more than half an hour to enter, search and clear a village, further highlighting the minimal interference of *Acorn* operations on the local people's lives.

Lesson 24

The complexity of insurgency warfare requires the counter-insurgency combatant to balance the elimination of the enemy with the maintenance of the loyalty or neutrality of the indigenous population. Poorly thought out operations that antagonise the local population will increase a mission's difficulty, enhance the insurgency's support among the indigenous people, and facilitate the enemy's recruitment of new members.

Acorn 46 was a typical operation. On 26 May 1969 a detachment of 1 Division Intelligence Unit with Vietnamese officers from the Hoa Long National Police travelled to the nearby hamlet of Ap Tay where they arrested three individuals. All three were money couriers who regularly carried currency to a VC camp in the province's north-west near Route 15. All were women, had sons serving with the VC, and were members of the communist Women's Liberation Association. The women were taken into custody for joint interrogation by provincial intelligence officers and 1 Division Intelligence Unit.

Acorn operations represented a sensible evolution of the cordon and search mission. Their benefits were obvious: a better targeted attack on the VC's infrastructure and less disruption to the lives of ordinary villagers. However, the task force's ability to undertake these missions did have significant prerequisites. *Acorn* operations required the Australians and Vietnamese to cooperate across language and procedure boundaries, and demanded the creation of a security environment in which the local people were willing to volunteer information on insurgents or sympathisers who might also be their neighbours.

THE ADVISER WAR

In 1962 Australia agreed to a request from the United States for the provision of military advisers to help the GVN in its struggle against the communist insurgency. The initial commitment, consisting of 30 officers and senior non-commissioned officers (NCOs), was organised into a unit named the Australian Army Training Team Vietnam (AATTV) or, as it was better known, 'The Team'. Its first commander was Australia's counter-insurgency expert, Colonel F. P. (Ted) Serong. The AATTV's arrival in Vietnam heralded the larger ground deployment that would occur in 1965.

Colonel F. P. (Ted) Serong, the AATTV's first commander. Serong raised the unit in 1962 and led it until 1965.
AWM P01508.001.

The Australians joined a rapidly expanding body of American advisers. Serong allocated his team widely, but mainly in the I Corps Area in the north. He distributed his soldiers as follows: 10 men to the Vietnamese National Training Centre in Phu Bai; 10 men to the Civil Guard and Self Defence Corps Training Centre at Hiep Khanh; 4 men to the Ranger Training Centre at Duc My; 2 men to the CIA Program at Da Nang. Serong and the rest of the team made up the headquarters in Saigon.

Initially the Australian rules of engagement limited the AATTV's role specifically to training in jungle warfare techniques, village defence and advanced skills such as communications. The government did not allow its advisers to go on operations with the units that they assisted. However, this restriction proved unsatisfactory. The credibility of the Australian advisers suffered in the eyes of the South Vietnamese because the instructors were not exposed to the same degree of risk as their students. Moreover, it was incorrect to assume that training could be limited to a classroom experience. School-centred training was only one stage in the transfer of higher military skills. The AATTV members had to observe and instruct their students in the field if they were to share the full range of their knowledge. In addition, field experience was necessary for the Australians if they were to ascertain the extent of their success as advisers and confirm the validity of their syllabus in the cauldron of battle. AATTV personnel needed first hand experience in observing the enemy in order to make any required adjustments to their instruction and compensate for the VC's reaction to the enhancement of South Vietnamese fighting capabilities.

Lesson 25

Advisers must be drawn from the most capable soldiers in the force. They must be masters of their trade, excellent communicators, and cognisant of other cultures and values. Lastly, they must earn the respect of those they teach if their instruction is to have lasting value.

The final rationale for changing the AATTV's rules of engagement was due to the high regard in which they were held. Wilton believed Australia's advisers could be more profitably employed if the government lifted their restrictions.

In mid-1964 the government expanded the AATTV's tasks to include advisory duties on operations. Accompanying the switch was an expansion of the unit, first to 83 and then 100 personnel. As the reinforcements arrived, Serong posted them to ARVN field units, Regional Force and Popular Force training centres, and CIA programs. The move to operational advising brought with it a considerable increase in risk, graphically illustrated by the death of WO2 Kevin Conway on 6 July 1964 during the defence of

Nam Dong Special Forces Camp. The shift in the AATTV's focus also resulted in team members effectively serving in leadership roles, commanding platoons and companies of South Vietnamese and tribal units. In their capacity as operational advisers, four members of the AATTV received Australia's highest decoration, the Victoria Cross.

For most AATTV members their tour of Vietnam must have been an isolating experience. Invariably, the Australians worked singly, or at best as pairs, in an advisory team that was mainly American. The two allies did not always share the same training philosophy and Team members had to advance their own ideas while still working within an American-dominated system. Not surprisingly, American training priorities stressed the rapid movement of large numbers of troops, and the application of huge volumes of artillery and air power. American trainers emphasised war on the massive scale, both in the offensive and the defensive. Naturally, the Australians took a less grand approach in the direction of their instruction. Australian advisers preferred to focus on bushcraft, ambush and counter-ambush, platoon tactics and individual combat skills. AATTV soldiers put more stress than the Americans chose to on the need for units to patrol constantly and, most importantly, to be patient. For example, when Captain Barry Tinkler arrived at the Civil Guard and Self Defence Corps Training Centre he rewrote the centre's training program and shifted its focus to small unit tactics and patrolling.

By 1965 the Team's three core areas of responsibility had become Special Forces advisers, ARVN advisers and Territorial Forces advisers. Special Forces advisers were effectively the commanders of units belonging to the Civilian Irregular Defence Group whose soldiers were drawn from indigenous ethnic groups that inhabited South Vietnam's central plateau and northern regions. Of these, the Montagnards comprised the most common nationality. ARVN advisers served attached to South Vietnamese infantry battalions and worked with the unit's commander and company officers. Their primary tasks were to train the officers in infantry tactics as well as technical skills such as radio management, and artillery and air support procedures. Territorial Force advisers worked with the GVN's local defence forces, the Regional Force and Popular Force. Their focus was on section- and platoon-level tactics, and the procedures required to obtain air and gun support.

While I Corps remained the Team's primary geographical focus, its members could be found anywhere in Vietnam. For example, in 1970 the unit had 93 members scattered among 16 provinces. The Team's distribution was: I Corps Area – 48; II Corps Area – 16; III Corps Area – 17; and IV Corps Area – 12.

WO2 Laurie Jackson, AATV, instructs a Vietnamese signaller in Thua Thien Province, 1969.
AWM LES/69/0420/VN.

Major P. J. Badcoe, VC.
AWM 116857.

For most of the war the Team had a minimal presence in Phuoc Tuy, the home of 1 ATF. It need not have been this way. In 1967, Westmoreland offered the COMAFV, Major-General D. Vincent, the opportunity to take over the adviser responsibilities in the province from the Americans. Vincent, in turn, raised the matter with the Chairman of the Chief of Staffs Committee, Wilton, and the CGS, Lieutenant-General Thomas Daly. Two ATF Commanders, Jackson and Graham, supported the adviser takeover. They argued that if Australians replaced the Americans at Ba Ria the task force would have greater influence over provincial authorities and on the direction of counter-insurgency efforts in Phuoc Tuy. In addition, Australian advisers would teach the province's territorial units 1 ATF combat procedures instead of American ones, thereby simplifying joint operations between the two forces.

WO2 Ray Simpson, VC (left), enjoys a beer in Saigon with his fellow VC winner WO2 Keith Payne.
AWM LES/69/0590/VN.

In the end, the Australians declined Westmoreland's offer. A takeover of Phuoc Tuy advisory tasks would have required a significant increase in Australia's commitment to Vietnam. The American headquarters in Phuoc Tuy numbered over 100 personnel, not including the advisers serving in the field. The Australian Army did not have the available personnel, nor did the government want to accept the necessary increase in expenditure. In addition, a relocation of the Team to Phuoc Tuy would have disrupted the existing advisory effort which was functioning well. AATTV personnel had established ties and commitments to the areas in which they were already working. Any transfer to Phuoc Tuy risked Australia's hard-won achievements and the respect they had garnered amongst the ARVN elsewhere in Vietnam, especially in the critical I Corps Area.

The reluctance of the government and the army's senior officers to take over Phuoc Tuy's advisory tasks pitted the strategic and operational levels of war against each other. For the government and the senior officers, the AATTV's dispersal gave Australia a Vietnam-wide presence that provided an independent assessment of the progress of the war. If the team's relocation had taken place it would have dramatically narrowed Australia's access to information and increased its dependence on American-developed and -sanctioned reports. By contrast, from the perspective of Jackson and Graham, the Team's relocation would have been a step towards greater Australian operational control of the province. One of the chronic handicaps under which 1 ATF fought was the lack of a single strategy and commonality of effort in the prosecution of counter-insurgency war against Phuoc Tuy's VC. The replacement of American with Australian advisers would not have immediately resulted in a single war effort, but it represented a move in that direction. The Team did post a handful of advisers who served in Ba Ria where they provided liaison between GVN officials and 1 ATF at Nui Dat.

The relocation of the AATTV received a more public review in early 1971. Journalist Denis Warner raised the issue in an article in Brisbane's *Courier Mail* newspaper. However, any takeover of advisory responsibilities still required a daunting increase in personnel, an unpalatable step especially since 1 ATF's drawdown would begin later in the year. Moreover, at this stage in the war, the opportunity for 1 ATF to gain an operational benefit from the Team's presence in Phuoc Tuy had long passed.

It was not until later in Australia's commitment that the Team gained a significant role as advisers in Phuoc Tuy through the Mobile Advisory and Training Teams (MATT) concept. The United States had initiated MATT at the end of 1967. The Australians were to take over from American teams already operating in Phuoc Tuy. The Prime Minister, John Gorton, announced the formation of the Australian MATT on 22 April 1970.

1 ATF had provided some training of provincial units as one of its regular responsibilities. However, this instruction was undertaken on an ad hoc basis by units whenever they could task personnel from other duties. Usually the training team was a temporary secondment by a party of Australian soldiers to, for example, a Regional Force Company. Training South Vietnamese soldiers was an extra duty for the units based at Nui Dat in much the same way as the task force's civic action scheme.

The MATT initiative allowed the Australians to place the training of provincial units onto a regular footing undertaken by troops dedicated to that mission. In April 1970 the AATTV raised 12 MATT teams, each consisting of 2 warrant officers and 4 corporals. At its peak the Australian MATT program comprised 14 teams. In addition, the AATTV established and manned the Vietnamese Jungle Warfare Training Centre at Nui Dat with a staff of 41. The AATTV's establishment expanded to 201 to accommodate its new duties.

WO2 RAYENE STUART SIMPSON, VC

Rayene Simpson was born in Chippendale in February 1926. He served in Korea and Malaya before joining the SAS in 1957. In 1962 Simpson was among the first warrant officers chosen for the newly formed AATTV.

In 1969 Simpson was on his third tour with the AATTV, commanding 232 Mobile Strike Force Company in Kontum Province. On 6 May 1969 one of his platoons came under heavy fire. Simpson formed up the rest of the company and led them in a flanking manoeuvre to relieve the pinned platoon. During the advance an Australian warrant officer, M. W. Gill, was seriously wounded. Without regard for his own safety, Simpson rushed out under heavy fire to retrieve him. He then returned to lead an assault and fought to within ten metres of the enemy's position. With darkness falling, and the enemy heavily entrenched, he provided covering fire while his company disengaged.

Five days later, in a different contact, Simpson again moved forward while under heavy machine-gun fire to rescue a wounded Australian and several indigenous soldiers. Simpson brought the men back and then held off the enemy's attacks until their evacuation.

Simpson was awarded the VC for his acts of 'personal bravery' and 'conspicuous gallantry' during this operation. He died in 1978.

WO2 Kevin Arthur 'Dasher' Wheatley, VC.
AWM 044438.

The MATTs in Phuoc Tuy were in fact not mobile. Australia created so many MATTs that, with some exceptions, they remained with the Regional Force unit to which they were first assigned. The MATT moved in with the Vietnamese, helping them defend their position while also providing their training. The MATT's roles covered both training and assistance on operations, and the syllabus included topics such as field defences, booby traps, patrolling, ambushing and minor infantry tactics. The Australians also covered methods of obtaining artillery, air strike and medical evacuation assistance.

The MATT instructors discovered that most of their students had only rudimentary military skills. Procedures which had become second nature to the Australians, for example, the conduct of a briefing prior to an operation, had to be explained. The advisers had to begin with the basics, such as showing the proper way to fill a sand bag and how to erect a wire barrier. Some units responded well, others showed little if any improvement. For example, the AATTV gave up on 302 Regional Force Battalion after six months of no progress, and redeployed its MATT elsewhere.

The legacy of the MATT concept is mixed. In February 1971 the Regional Force units in Phuoc Tuy participated in Operation *Dong Khoi*. This operation represented a nationwide effort aimed at VC infrastructure. The Regional Force units went into the field, but caught few VC. According to the AATTV's historian, Ian McNeill, it appeared as if the Vietnamese planners dispatched their forces to randomly chosen areas with no assessment of the probability of the enemy's presence. Unsurprisingly, this resulted in few contacts.

Private Reg Lillywhite, 6 RAR, demonstrates the M26 grenade to a group of Vietnamese interpreters in October 1966. Instructional duty was an extra task undertaken by 1 ATF's soldiers.
AWM CUN/66/0893/VN.

The MATT concept was a fine idea in principal, but it reflected a complete change in the American, and hence Australian, priorities. The Regional Force and Popular Force forces had been long neglected, often treated with disdain, and held at arm's length by 1 ATF. However, the low quality of the Regional Force and Popular Force was not all the fault of the Americans and Australians. Within the South Vietnamese hierarchy the Territorial Forces came last and were afflicted with incompetent, bored, and corrupt officers who led men lacking in interest, drive and motivation. A postwar assessment described the Territorial Forces as 'stepchildren' and commented that they were 'far down in priority for training, equipment, and leadership, resulting in marginal or unsatisfactory ratings in almost every category of their activities.'

The Australians long recognised the existence of a hierarchy of capability in Phuoc Tuy. The Australian troops were the province's elite soldiers while the Regional Force and Popular Force were best suited for static garrison duty. Now, with the assistance of the MATTs, the Australians were to transform the Regional Force and Popular Force into warriors who could take over the role of Phuoc Tuy's defenders when 1 ATF returned home. One MATT member commented that it was not possible to instil the necessary combat skills in the time permitted. Thirty days was not long enough to overcome years of neglect and create soldiers who were capable of defeating VC veterans in battle.

SUPPORTING THE ATF

The Raising of 1 Australian Logistic Support Company

The 1 RAR battalion group that Australia dispatched to Vietnam in 1965 included a logistic component called 1 Australian Logistic Support Company (1 ALSC). This was an ad hoc organisation that brought together elements from the Army's engineering, supply, transport, ordnance, medical and repair capabilities. Upon arrival at Bien Hoa, 1 ALSC joined the Support Battalion of the US 173 Airborne Brigade (Separate), and set up within the American formation's base area.

All the components of 1 ALSC were under tremendous pressure to ready themselves for their deployment, a process not helped by the lateness with which some elements received their notice for service in Vietnam. For example, the RAEME component—1

ALSC Workshop Detachment—was given just 18 days to form up and complete its preparations. Moreover, as it was specifically raised for this mission there were no extant establishment tables to guide its mobilisation. Instead, the Workshop Detachment received lists of items and required quantities page by page as they were drawn up, and the detachment's men worked late into the night by Coleman lamp pulling equipment and vehicles out of storage from warehouses at Holsworthy. Making the task even harder was that the drawing of stores took place in addition to numerous other training, administrative and force preparation tasks that the craftsmen had to complete.

For the first few months of the deployment, 1 ALSC struggled to meet demands made upon the unit's resources. This was a result of several assumptions that had been made in Canberra, and which would prove to have been overly optimistic. In part shortages occurred because 1 ALSC's equipment, maintenance and repair scales had been set too low and the unit consequently deployed with what was soon revealed as inadequate stocks. Shortages were exacerbated because planners expected that most of the unit's needs would be readily met by drawing on US Army depots. They had failed to appreciate fully the consequences of 1 RAR's deployment in the middle of the massive expansion of the United States' own forces in South Vietnam, and the pressure on the American support system to meet its requirements. In other cases shortages occurred because US equipment was not compatible with the Australian version: the oxyacetylene bottles used by the two forces had different thread patterns.

Lesson 26

The necessity of supply should not come as a surprise to an operation's planners. Logistic planning should commence simultaneously with operational planning and the two should be integrated at all levels. The requirements of support should not be treated as a hurried afterthought.

These initial problems were foreseeable, and should have been mitigated by the provision of additional supplies and equipment in the initial deployment, and a more robust rate of resupply. However, Australia has a long tradition of depending on a senior coalition partner for support, and the Army lacked the necessary experience in assessing its own operational requirements. The logistics of the Vietnam War would prove no different to that of previous conflicts.

The members of 1 ALSC worked hard to overcome their equipment deficiencies, while also helping to construct the Australian compound within the Bien Hoa base area. The arrival of additional stores on HMAS *Sydney* and the build-up of American capacity meant that shortages soon became manageable. However, Australian logistic officers often had to take matters into their own hands; they became proficient hagglers in the markets of Saigon. From local suppliers they purchased a diverse range of materials and services that included items such as office equipment, vehicles and parts, and engineering stores.

The Formation of 1 Australian Logistic Support Group

The decision to expand Australia's commitment in Vietnam to a task force size also necessitated an increase in the deployment's logistic organisation. This led to the raising of 1 Australian Logistic Support Group (1 ALSG), and its installation at the port of Vung Tau, on the shores of the South China Sea adjacent to Phuoc Tuy Province, and a short distance by road to Nui Dat.

A MK3 International delivers the beer ration to 7 RAR at Nui Dat. The sign reads: 'BEER TRUCK DO NOT DELAY'. AWM P01539.010.

A MK5 International Tipper being loaded with rolls of barbed wire. AWM P05330.001.

International 2½ ton and 5 ton Trucks

Mk 3 2½ Ton (Cargo)

Engine:
282 cubic inch 6 cylinder
BHP: 148
Transmission: 5 Speed
Fuel: Petrol
Wheel: 4 x 4
Dimensions:
621 x 244 x 251 mm
Wheel Base: 368 mm
GVW: 8,048 kg

Mk 5 5 Ton (Cargo)

Engine:
282 cubic inch 6 cylinder
BHP: 150
Transmission: 5 Speed
Fuel: Petrol
Wheel: 6 x 6
Dimensions:
645 x 241 x 302 mm
Wheel Base: 377 mm
GVW: 11,567 kg

In 1965 the mainstay of the Australian Army's transport fleet was the International Mk 3 2½ ton truck. The vehicle had been designed by ADE and built at the International Harvester plant in Dandenong. The Mk 3's limited capacity—the tip version was derisively known as the 'teaspoon tipper'— led to its progressive replacement in 1966 by the newer and larger Mk 5 model. The Internationals came in a variety of versions although the most common were general service and tipper. When needed, 1 ATF and 1 ALSG could also obtain heavier transport vehicles from US sources.

Vung Tau was the logical location for 1 ALSG, due to its proximity to 1 ATF and the port's development as a major United States military support facility. However, when its first commander Lieutenant Colonel D. L. Rouse arrived with his advance party at 1 ALSG's future location on the eastern shore of the Vung Tau Peninsula he found a 'green field' site that required an enormous amount of infrastructure improvements. He described the Australian sector of the base as primitive even by army standards, filthy and fly blown, and composed of sand dunes that constantly shifted in the wind. Vung Tau's terrain and the local weather pattern dictated that for six months of the year the compound was buffered by wind-borne sand, and for the other half of the year saturated by monsoonal rains and humidity. These conditions would be mediated, but only after considerable engineering work.

Rouse had also been unnecessarily handicapped by the short notice of his appointment—just three weeks and inadequate consultation on what units his command needed. Consequently, Army Headquarters overlooked some requirements: 1 ALSG did not originally contain a Field Hygiene Unit, an inexplicable oversight given the deployment's location in South-East Asia. Moreover, 1 ALSG's assigned establishment bore no rational relation to its responsibilities, and most probably represented the number of personnel positions available for the support staff after Army Headquarters had filled 1 ATF's and HQ AFV's requirements.

Despite the experience gained from the raising of the support company the previous year, Australia would again deploy a logistic organisation with inadequate initial stocks, and would betray over-optimistic expectations of their augmentation from allied sources. In fact, Rouse's advance party was so poorly prepared that it had to fossick tentage from an American salvage dump. As materials arrived from Australia there was no place to store them, nor even mechanical equipment to off-load the trucks that transported the supplies from the port. Instead, the equipment was pinch barred off truck-beds and stacked on the sand. The wind quickly blew the sand out from under the piles of crates or pallets, however, sending them crashing to the ground. Once storage tents arrived, soldiers had to take care to keep the flaps secured, otherwise the ever present wind removed the sand from under the poles causing the tent to collapse. Hard stands were non-existent and the tradesmen carried out their work directly on the sand. Consequently, sand filtered into engines and transmissions, while moisture penetrated sights and radios, and bamboo wrecked tires and tracks, all of which greatly increased maintenance requirements.

1 ALSG base at Vung Tau, as it appeared in 1966.
AWM MISC/66/0025/VN.

Once the rains arrived 1 ALSG's problems with the sand eased, only to be replaced by chronic flooding. For example, the work area for 101 Field Workshop was in a small valley between two sandhills and sat just above the water table. With the rains the water table rose and soon the craftsmen negotiated their work site on punts made from pallets. This problem was solved only by raising the height of the valley floor by more than a metre, a task accomplished by bulldozing vast quantities of sand off the surrounding hills and onto the lower lying ground.

In fact, the Australians had to modify the topography of the entire base area in order to make it useable. This was a massive engineering effort that saw the shifting of hills to fill lagoons and build up work areas so that they sat sufficiently high above the water table. On top of the now levelled sand, the tip trucks of 87 Transport Platoon dumped tons of crushed rock which the engineers from 17 Construction Squadron used to form hard stands upon which equipment could safely be stored and workshops and buildings constructed.

Of course, while 1 ALSG built a base it also undertook its other task of supporting 1 ATF, and it is a testimony to their labours that the logisticians were able to accomplish both jobs. Gradual improvements were thus made in 1 ALSG's work areas, and in March 1968 an inspection report observed that the area bore little resemblance to what had existed two years previously.

The Australian base at Vung Tau after improvements in 1967.
AWM P01721.015

Managing the Supply Chain

The Australians in Vietnam obtained their support from three distinct sources. They were:

- United States depots in theatre;
- South Vietnamese government and contractor entities; and
- The national support base in Australia.

Each of these sources was critical for the maintenance of 1 ATF's operational capability.

It was government policy that the national support base only provide equipment and supplies that were not otherwise available from in-theatre sources. In practice this meant that only Australian-specific items came from home, for example, 20-pounder ammunition for the Centurion tanks which, being of British origin, were not in use with the US Army. The government implemented this policy as it simplified the deployment's maintenance and reduced the cost of sea and air shipping which would have been needed if all materials had to be sourced from Australia. In many cases the Americans themselves delivered the required supplies to Nui Dat, thereby eliminating the need to accept, store and issue the items at Vung Tau. For example, the US Army Depot at Long Binh—the source of Australian rations, engineers and ordnance items of US origin—was 45 miles by road to Nui Dat. Standardisation with US weapons also increased compatibility between the US and Australian forces, thus making in theatre support easier. In addition to equipment the Australian contingent had ready access to American transportation services, and US trucks and helicopters readily moved Australian troops, equipment and supplies.

TABLE 4
Source of Australian Supply (main items)

Stores Category	United States Source	Australian Source
Engineer	Defence stores, construction materials, plumbing and electrical fittings, air conditioning, kitchen equipment	Plant, special project stores, generation, refrigeration, air conditioning, assault boats, prefab huts
Signals	Poles, cables	Fixed communications equipment, cryptic equipment, radio crystals
Rations	Fresh rations, combat rations	Combat, composite and tinned equivalent rations
POL	Fuels and lubricants	Australian specific lubricants
Medical and Dental	All medical and dental stores except special items	Special items
Canteen	Some tinned foodstuffs, liquors	Tinned foodstuffs, beer, soft drinks, luxury items
Ordnance	Most types of ammunition, repair and replacement parts for US origin equipment, general stores	Tank and 9mm ammunition, clothing, weapons, batteries, radio equipment, repair parts for vehicles

Once the US and Australian supply systems had geared up, the need for urgent or ad hoc purchases from South Vietnamese sources declined. However, the South Vietnamese continued to provide the Australians with labour and certain services under contract, such as laundry services. Vietnamese labourers were not allowed at Nui Dat for operational security reasons. This prohibition did not extend to Vung Tau, where the US forces made extensive use of local labour. While it is likely that some of the workers in Australian employ at Vung Tau were also in the pay of the Viet Cong, the American policy on local labour had already compromised the base's security. Approximately 500 Vietnamese were employed by the Australian Civil Labour Unit while an additional 130 worked for the AFV Amenities Unit.

Landing Ship Medium (LSM)

Construction: Steel
Length: 62.03 m
Breadth: 10.37 m
Engines:
  Two Fairbanks Morse Marine Diesel, 2880 bhp
Cruising Speed: 11.5 knots
Range: 7250 km
Cargo Capacity:
  Five MBT, or Twelve 2.5 ton GS Vehicles, or 270 tons dwt
Armament:
  one 40 mm Bofors and several .50 inch machine guns
Crew:
  Four Officers, 46 ORs

In 1959 Australia purchased four mothballed LSMs from the United States Navy. They were designated AV1353 *Harry Chauvel*; AV1354 *Brudenell White*; AV1355 *Vernon Sturdee*; and AV1356 *Clive Steele* and formed into 32 Small Ship Squadron. The vessels provided the Australian Army with a blue-water heavy lift capacity until their disposal in 1971. The only LSM to sustain battle damage during the Vietnam War was the *Clive Steele* when it was hit by three rockets on 5 January 1969. The ship was slightly damaged and there were no casualties.

The Clive Steele under repair at Vung Tau. A new screw is to be fitted.
AWM MISC/69/0277/VN.

Nearly all personnel, equipment and stores sourced from Australia arrived at Vung Tau by sea. The RAAF did provide a regular C130 service, but its limited capacity allowed only for the shipment of high priority items. Sea transit was provided by a number of assets, and included vessels belonging to the RAN, Australian Army and contractors. In 1963 the RAN recommissioned the *Sydney* as fast troop transport, modifying it from its former role as an aircraft carrier. During the war the ship made 24 passages, carrying units and their vehicles and stores. The Army's 32 Small Ship Squadron provided four LSMs. These vessels were used as heavy lift ships, transporting tanks and heavy engineering equipment. Once in theatre they also provided intra-theatre lift, and were often tasked to transport American vehicles and equipment. The Army also had its own cargo ship, the 1100 ton cargo capacity *John Monash*, which made several runs between Australia and Vung Tau.

Most cargo arrived at Vung Tau either on the MV *Jeparit* or MV *Boonaroo*. Both ships had been chartered by the Department of Shipping and Transport on behalf of the Army. The *Jeparit* made 38 trips and the *Boonaroo* two. Both ships suffered from industrial action. For its second voyage the RAN had to commission the *Boonaroo* and provide it with a navy crew. After the voyage it was decommissioned. The *Jeparit* made 21 passages to Vietnam with a mixed RAN and Merchant Marine crew. However, in December 1969 after further industrial action, the government took over the vessel, which made its remaining 17 voyages as HMAS *Jeparit*. The government also chartered vessels as needed. For example, the Centurion tanks returned to Australia over three trips on the Japanese *Harma Maru*.

Command and Control

The most intractable obstacle to the provision of efficient support in theatre was the deployment's logistic command and control arrangements. For nearly the entire period of Australian military presence in Vietnam there was no single officer responsible for the overall provision and coordination of logistics.

Lesson 27

The combat arms' maxim of unity of command also applies equally to the support arms. Effective logistics requires effective command and control.

It might be expected that the officer holding the position of Commander 1 ALSG was the deployment's supreme logistic commander. This was not the case, however, and often the position's holder was a relatively junior officer with the rank of merely a lieutenant colonel, although colonels and brigadiers also served in this appointment. The reality was that the Commander 1 ALSG was responsible only for the local administration of Vung Tau and the administration of the units that worked at the base. In effect, he served as a coordinating authority, and it was at a daily coordination conference that the various representatives of the logistic corps set the priorities for current and future support tasks. Neither did the Commander 1 ALSG have any responsibility over the RAN and RAAF service elements that were also at Vung Tau.

In Saigon, on the staff of HQ AFV, there were several logistic officers representing each of the corps. They served as logistic advisers to the COMAFV, oversaw support contract arrangements with MACV and the GVN, and served as the technical representatives for their respective corps. Their positions were completely independent from the Commander of 1 ALSG. Moreover, the RAN and RAAF maintained their own support staffs in Saigon, and these were separate from the Army.

Over time, as 1 ATF's base at Nui Dat became more established, it gained its own logistic capability. This consisted either of detachments drawn from the support units established at Vung Tau or in some cases entire units deployed specifically for 1 ATF's direct support. The growth of a support organisation at Nui Dat did make operational sense. For example, the availability of the tanks and helicopters was increased by there being at Nui Dat a dedicated repair and refuelling capability, which meant that these high-demand vehicles and aircraft did not have to return to Vung Tau for resupply or maintenance. However, the existence of a forward logistic base also created considerable duplication of effort, encouraged an excess of manpower, and resulted in the need to maintain workshops and depots in both Vung Tau and Nui Dat. For what was in effect only a brigade size deployment, this represented a considerable excess of support. In addition, the need to maintain forward elements caused administrative difficulties for support units that also had to maintain detachments in two locations. Unfortunately, since the Commander 1 ALSG did not have any authority at Nui Dat it was impossible to rationalise or coordinate the logistic support between the two Australian bases.

The fracturing of Australia's supply infrastructure into several nodes, and the absence of an overall support commander, resulted in a needlessly complex logistic system. A rationalisation of the logistic command and control would have allowed for a more efficient provision of support to all deployed elements, no matter their location, or even their service. However, this goal was not achieved until the deployment's final days, and only once the contingent's numbers had already greatly contracted.

Medical and Nursing Support to the ATF

Throughout 1 RAR's attachment to 173 Airborne Brigade (Separate) Australia largely relied on the United States for the medical support of its troops. The deployment contained only a handful of medical officers, and seriously injured Australian troops received treatment at a United States hospital at Clark Air Force Base in the Philippines. In 1966, with the expansion of the

170

Australian commitment, the government decided to provide 1 ATF with its own integral medical capacity. In May 1966, 2 Field Ambulance established itself at Vung Tau as a part of 1 ASLG. The following year it was replaced by 8 Field Ambulance which also set up a limited treatment facility at Nui Dat. As 1 ATF continued to expand so did its medical support, culminating in the opening of 1 Australian Field Hospital at Vung Tau.

Over the course of their service in Vietnam the force's medical personnel treated over 1900 battle injuries, approximately 2650 non-battle injuries and more than 16,000 disease admissions at these facilities. In addition, there were more than 11,000 recorded cases of venereal disease. Precise figures are not available due to poor statistical reporting of treatment.

The deployment's public health capability was enhanced with the arrival of a detachment of soldiers from 1 Field Hygiene Company in 1968. Field Hygiene personnel were responsible for the control of disease carriers—especially malarial mosquitoes and rodents—the maintenance of sanitary standards, and the security and purity of the Australian water supply.

Nurse Lieutenant Margaret Ahern on a Medcap visit to the village of Hoa Long.
AWM GIL/67/0483/VN.

A number of civilian medical teams also served in Vietnam. These personnel provided medical aid to the South Vietnamese people, serving under a SEATO aid program that was administered by the then Department of External Affairs. These doctors, nurses and associated medical professionals were drawn from medical facilities from across Australia. In Vietnam they served at hospitals at Long Xuyen (1964-1970), in the Delta; Bien Hoa (1966-1972), near Saigon; Vung Tau (1966-1970); and briefly in Ba Ria (late 1968–early 1969).

The only Australian female military personnel to serve in Vietnam were the nurses of the Royal Australian Army Nursing Corps (RAANC) and the Royal Australian Air Force Nursing Service (RAAFNS). The first four RAANC sisters arrived at Vung Tau in May 1967 where they joined 8 Field Ambulance. After the raising of 1 Australian Field Hospital, the number of nurses gradually increased, peaking at twelve, including two New Zealand sisters. While nurses primarily spent their time at Vung Tau they also participated in 1 ATF's Medcap program, thereby helping to provide basic medical and preventative care to villagers across Phuoc Tuy Province. Over the course of the conflict 43 RAANC sisters served in South Vietnam.

After the establishment of the Task Force it became government policy to evacuate to Australia for further treatment and rehabilitation wounded personnel who could not readily be returned to duty at Vung Tau. Transfer was by air and patient care was the responsibility of the sisters of the RAAFNS. The RAAF provided a regular fortnightly C130 evacuation service that transited to Australia via RAAF Base Butterworth in Malaysia. The medical evacuation nurses usually spent only a few hours at Vung Tau, while the patients were loaded. Over the course of the conflict the RAAF evacuated over 3,200 casualties, including nearly 200 New Zealanders.

A lesser known RAAFNS contribution to Australia's role in the Vietnam War were the sisters who flew out of Clark Air Force Base in the Philippines with USAF 902 Medical Evacuation Squadron. Between July 1966 and April 1971 a total of 32 RAAF nurses worked on USAF C130 and C118A aircraft, caring for wounded US personnel on the flight from Vietnam to the Philippines. Unlike their colleagues who worked the evacuation route to Australia, these sisters did not just fly in and out of Vung Tau but covered the length and breadth of Vietnam, picking up and caring for casualties from locations that included Saigon, Da Nang, Cam Ran Bay and Qui Nhon.

Homeward Bound

As Australia withdrew from Vietnam it was the job of 1 ALSG to return home the Army's equipment, vehicles and stores. This process commenced in 1970 when the Australian government decided to reduce 1 ATF to a two-battalion task force and to withdraw the tanks. The extraction of the Australians from Phuoc Tuy and Vung Tau would prove an equally laborious and demanding a task as the deployment.

As units departed Nui Dat they transitioned to Vung Tau in preparation for the return to Australia. The staff of 1 ALSG had to account for and prepare for shipment virtually all of the equipment in theatre that the Australian government did not intend to hand over to the government of South Vietnam. This meant that all equipment had to be inventoried, cleaned, restored, preserved, packed and labelled so that it could be safely loaded onto ships and returned to its correct unit or warehouse location in Australia. In addition, all returning items had to meet customs and quarantine requirements, and the government dispatched a customs team to Vung Tau to provide assistance. The government also installed a health team at Vung Tau in order to safeguard against the introduction into Australia of any exotic diseases or contaminated goods.

The task of returning the force's equipment and stores to Australia was enormous. After an initial period of shortage, the Australian supply system had built up a capacity that meant an excess of munitions, equipment and stores of all kinds was now held in Vung Tau. In part, this was because the supply system employed by both the United States and Australia during the Vietnam War was of the 'push system' nature. This meant that replacement issues of stores arrived on a regular basis from depots in theatre or from the Australian national base without units needing to place a demand. Unfortunately, programmed usage rates could vary tremendously from actual usage rates, which meant that surplus stocks built up quickly. In addition, the Australian supply system tended to be inflexible so that it was difficult to modify or cease the dispatch of items that were either no longer needed or already present at Vung Tau in sufficient numbers. For example, well after the preparation of the Centurion Tanks for return to Australia had commenced, spare parts continued to arrive at Vung Tau.

A further complication in the return of materials to Australia was the sheer number of line items that are held by a modern military organisation. For example, 1 Advanced Ordnance Depot held over 16,000 line items and 55 Engineering Stores held a similar number. The term 'line items' does not represent the volume of materials but the number of different types of items, every one of which the personnel of 1 ALSG had to individually inventory.

The preparation of vehicles for their return to Australia was also a time-consuming and challenging exercise. All vehicles had to be cleaned in order to prevent the introduction of exotic and potentially dangerous or economically ruinous flora and fauna into Australia. Cleaning personnel had to remove all traces of dirt from the vehicles, a task undertaken with small brushes and water hoses. It took, on average:

- 4000 gallons of water and 20 to 30 man hours to clean a Land Rover;
- 10000 gallons of water and 35 to 55 man hours to clean an APC; and
- 15000 gallons of water and 156 man hours to clean a tank.

Overall, the Australians had to clean over 1300 vehicles.

THE LOSS OF VIETNAM

The Effect of Tet

As South Vietnam celebrated Tet—the Lunar New Year holiday— VC forces broke the agreed ceasefire and launched a massive offensive across the entire country. The offensive commenced on 30 January 1968 and, over the next few days, saw attacks on Saigon, 36 of 44 provincial capitals, and 64 of 242 district towns.

1 ATF played an important, albeit peripheral, role in the repulse of the communist forces. On 22 January, Hughes had attended a conference at HQ II FFV at Long Binh. The American commander and Hughes's operational superior, Lieutenant-General Frederick Weyand, asked his subordinate to bring the task force to Bien Hoa to help protect the airfield and the nearby base area of Long Binh in anticipation of VC rocket attacks.

The Australians designated the assignment Operation *Coburg*. It was to be the largest Australian operation to date, involving initially 2 and 7 RAR, and support arms. 3 RAR later replaced 7 RAR. In addition, a detachment of 1 ALSG deployed to Long Binh to provide support to the AO. Operation *Coburg* was notable for the VC's attack on FSB Anderson on 18 February. This was the first time an Australian FSB had come under assault, and 7 RAR handily repulsed the attackers.

1 ATF's third battalion, 3 RAR, recently arrived in Vietnam, remained at Nui Dat to protect the base while continuing its acclimatisation. At first light on 1 February, *D445 Provincial Mobile Battalion* occupied the Phuoc Tuy capital of Ba Ria. The same morning Nui Dat came under a brief and ineffective mortar barrage that was possibly a diversion. To assist the hard-pressed garrison, 1 ATF dispatched to Ba Ria a relief force consisting of A Company, 3 RAR, supported by the APCs of 3 Troop A Squadron 3 Cavalry Regiment. After intense fighting they succeeded in regaining the town by mid-afternoon of 2 February. The Australians inflicted heavy casualties on *D445 Provincial Mobile Battalion* and accounted for 40 enemy KIA at a cost of 18 WIA. The VC also attacked the nearby village of Long Dien, east of Ba Ria. Over several days 3 RAR supported local South Vietnamese units in searching and clearing the village.

Hanoi's objective in the Tet offensive was to spark a widespread rebellion against the Thieu regime which they hoped would lead to its replacement by a more centralist government which would demand an American withdrawal. At great cost to themselves— approximately 45,000 casualties—the communists completely failed to achieve their goal. Except for Hue, American, Australian and South Vietnamese troops quickly recaptured all of the cities and towns that the communists had seized. Hue held out till 25 February before its recapture by units of the USMC and the ARVN. By the end of February the communist leaders had accepted defeat and ordered their forces to cease large-scale attacks. One North Vietnamese officer recorded that after Tet, 'our organisations were shaken to the roots...'.

Tet was the turning point of the American war in Vietnam. Yet, oddly, despite their savage losses, the communists were the ones who emerged as victors while it was the Americans who tasted defeat. The aftermath of Tet showed that victory or defeat is more than a comparison of casualties suffered or inflicted and territory won or lost. War has a psychological dimension, and it was the wider perception of the battle's outcome that transformed battlefield success into strategic failure and defeat.

The United States military lost the aura of victory even as its soldiers slaughtered the enemy's forces. The communist attack had not come as a surprise, and MACV had implemented countermeasures to the pending threat. 1 ATF's transfer to Bien Hoa had been part of the American preparations for the communist attack. However, what caught the American command by surprise was the magnitude of the enemy's onslaught. Just four days before Tet's commencement Westmoreland had confidently reported to Johnson that the previous year had seen the enemy forced from the south's population centres. The MACV commander went on to conclude that the VC were in irreversible decline. No one in Saigon or Washington had conceived that the enemy possessed the professionalism, organisation, resources and manpower to undertake an attack of such complexity and scale. The reality stunned America's military and political leaders.

Even more important was the American public's reaction to Tet. Periodic assurances by the White House and MACV of the growing success of the American strategy of attrition now rang hollow. Instead, news reports featuring the seizure of the American Embassy in Saigon and pitched battles in the city's streets suggested that the communists' will was unbroken and that victory remained elusive and distant. The subsequent revelation that the report of the Embassy's capture was false, and that the street fighting was easily defeated, did little to restore American confidence in the war's direction.

Unskilled Machiavellian machinations by Westmoreland and the Chairman of the Joint Chiefs of Staff, General Earle Wheeler, further inflamed American opinion against the war. Wheeler hatched a plan to force Johnson to activate the Army Reserve, a step the President had so far refused to take. Wheeler suggested to Westmoreland that MACV demand large reinforcements, not to recover from Tet, but to expand the war to the enemy's sanctuaries in Laos and Cambodia against a weakened opponent before Hanoi replaced its enormous losses.

An APC from B Squadron 3 Cavalry Regiment manoeuvres itself out of a bog. In Phuoc Tuy, Australian armour proved its ability to operate in myriad types of terrain. AWM BEL/69/0512/VN.

Westmoreland settled on the figure of 206,000 more men, a 40 per cent increase that would bring the American commitment in Vietnam to over 730,000. The request, leaked to the press shortly after its arrival at the White House, fuelled a storm of controversy. On a superficial level Westmoreland's appeal for reinforcements seemed like an admission of defeat, and in the process all parties overlooked MACV's proposed operational change of focus.

To most observers the need for massive reinforcements conflicted with the previously positive assessments that had come from MACV, and seemed to confirm Walter Cronkite's conclusion that negotiation was the only way out of an unwinnable quagmire. Moreover, MACV remained unable to enunciate a clear plan for victory. After Tet, the new Secretary of Defense, Clark Clifford, requested from the army an outline of its strategy in Vietnam. Clifford lampooned the military's reply as 'if we continue to pour troops in at some unknown rate and possibly in an unlimited number for an unknown period of time, that, ultimately, it was their opinion the enemy would have suffered that degree of attrition that would force the enemy to sue for some kind of peace.'

General Creighton Abrams, Westmoreland's successor as COMUSMACV. He is speaking to Sergeant Stuart Keys, Mortar Platoon, 9 RAR.
AWM COM/69/0026/VN.

Tet toppled America's wartime leadership. On 31 March 1968 Johnson addressed the nation on television to make two major announcements. First he stated that he was prepared 'to move immediately to peace through negotiations.' Then at the end of his speech he dropped the other bombshell—he would not seek or accept nomination for re-election as president. In June it was Westmoreland's turn. He was promoted out of MACV to take up the post of Army Chief of Staff. His replacement was his deputy General Creighton Abrams.

The part played by the media in transforming Tet from an American victory into a defeat has been hotly contested by military officers, scholars and members of the media. What is often forgotten in this debate, however, is that prior to Tet US public opinion had already begun to shift against the war. By the time of the communist offensive public support was below 50 percent. Moreover, the reporting on Tet did not accelerate the rate of decline in public support which remained steady for the rest of the war. More importantly, the apportionment of blame for the decline in public support for the war after Tet has helped to conceal a more important truth, one that the actions of the media had helped to reveal. Up until the onset of the communist offensive, the American public's expectations of victory in Vietnam derived from reports and pronouncements issued by MACV that exuded confidence and faith in its concept of war and strategy of attrition. MACV left little room for doubt that America was winning. Tet revealed that Westmoreland's claim of progress towards victory was unsubstantiated, and his faith in attrition misplaced. It showed that the North Vietnamese would bear the cost of attrition more readily and for longer than the Americans. Within the White House, the communist offensive made it uncomfortably apparent that after more than three years of conflict the United States did not have a viable strategy and that the prospect of victory was as distant a chimera in 1968 as it had been in 1965. In effect, the United States, the GVN, and their allies, including Australia, had become convinced of certain success by their own victory propaganda.

In May 1968 peace talks opened in Paris. In attendance were representatives of the United States, North Vietnam, GVN and the VC. At the same time the United States moved from an attitude of escalation to one of withdrawal and Vietnamisation. What Hanoi's leadership had not achieved on the Tet battlefields they gained at the peace talks. The United States had committed itself to withdrawing from South Vietnam, and while the war continued and more soldiers died, the communist leaders knew that victory and unification were theirs.

Was A Military Victory Possible?

It is all too easy to suggest that American, and hence Australian, defeat was inevitable in the Vietnam War. Indeed, counter-insurgency wars are among the hardest and longest conflicts to wage. However, such a suggestion implies that there was nothing the allies could have done to change a preordained outcome. 'What if' questions are always problematic for historians and this section does require the reader's indulgence for speculation. However, speculation permits the analysis of other options that could have changed the war's outcome.

Insurgency wars are complex conflicts and there were a number of political and military reasons for the allied defeat in Vietnam. Among the military factors was MACV's relentless pursuit of a flawed strategy and, to a lesser extent, 1 ATF's failure to resolve the inherent conflicts between the American and Australian concepts of war. American leaders approached the war as a conventional mid-intensity conflict and sought to win the war through the destruction of the VC's main force units. By contrast, the Australians arrived in South Vietnam with well-developed principles of counter-insurgency warfare, and were determined to achieve victory by winning the population's 'hearts and minds'. Of the three combatants, the VC were the ones whose concept of war best suited the requirements of the conflict.

Both the American and Australian concepts proved ill-considered choices for the character of the opponent and the nature of the environment in which their troops fought. The main flaw in the American and Australian concepts was that both directed their efforts against VC areas of strength rather than weakness. The result was that MACV struggled in vain to destroy an apparition, while the VC consistently evaded the massive blows directed against them and thereby successfully negated supposed American advantages in firepower, resources and technology. Through their ability to initiate combat at points and times of their own choosing, the VC made battle into an arena of strength that the Americans could not overcome.

Australian doctrine also sought to defeat the enemy at a point of great strength rather than weakness. Although 1 ATF was a ready participant in MACV's search and destroy operations, the Australians also believed it was necessary to target the insurgency's village-level infrastructure. The elimination of VC cadres and the village organisation, the Australians accepted, would lead indirectly to the destruction of VC's main force units.

However the VC laid down the foundation of their local level infrastructure in the 1930s, and had built on it ever since. By 1965 the Vietnam communist movement had penetrated deeply into the country's village structure. The communist penetration of local government was so broad and so widely accepted by the people that, to many peasants, the GVN was irrelevant. When the task force arrived in Phuoc Tuy they found a VC-dominated province. When the Australians left Phuoc Tuy 7 years later the VC's cadre and village organisation remained in place.

Lesson 28

Identify your enemy's weaknesses and focus on them. An opponent's weak points will crumble more readily than its strong points.

In war, it is generally easier to succeed if a combatant targets points of enemy weakness rather than strength. In Vietnam, the Americans and Australians did the opposite. While the American and Australian concepts were different, the two forces committed the same error in the application of their methods of waging the war. In addition, they persevered long after their doctrines had been found wanting, failing to seek a new way until it was too late.

Two questions remain. First, why did the Americans and Australians first choose, and then continue, to target enemy points of strength? Second, what could they have done differently that might have made victory possible?

The first question is the easier to answer. The American and Australian Armies entered the Vietnam War with existing doctrines in which they held great faith. In the face of failure their response, particularly that of the MACV, was invariably more of the same, only at a greater level of intensity. Compounding the problem for the Australians was the ongoing need to conform to American operational requirements. Institutionally, the two armies lacked mechanisms with which to test their faith, identify faults and incorporate adaptations. In short, at its core, both armies' failure in Vietnam was intellectual.

Lesson 29

If operations fail to achieve strategic goals, commanders must have the courage to assess existing procedures, the vision to seek new methods, and the strength to force change. Intensification of effort may be appropriate, but it may also be the refuge of the intellectually lazy.

Some Australian officers were aware that the task force's operational preferences were not leading towards victory. One COMAFV—Vincent—observed that large-scale sweeps of the countryside were ineffective and that a four- or five-man patrol paid a better return. In 1969, 5 RAR's historian, O'Neill, concluded that allied attempts to win the war by destroying the VC's main force units were doomed to failure. However, their judgements effected little overall change right up to the conflict's end. In mid-1971, for example, VC main force units moved back into northern Phuoc Tuy. In June, as Australia's deployment neared its end, 1 ATF embarked on Operation *Overlord*, one of the biggest search and destroy missions ever undertaken in the province. The result was the same: the VC melted away, reduced their activity in accordance with the phases of revolutionary conflict as defined in their concept of war, and bided their time for a little longer.

Regarding what could have been done differently, there were other options besides search and destroy or cordon and search operations, but the climate in Headquarters MACV and 1 ATF did not encourage a change in direction in Phuoc Tuy. One alternate approach was for the allies to focus on the interdiction of the VC's logistic network. Logistics was an area of VC weakness, especially at the nexus between the main force units and the village organisation. Each of the VC entities was mutually dependent on the other; but the link between the field force and the supporting village organisation had no inherent defensive capability. In 1968 O'Neill highlighted the value of interdiction operations aimed at the enemy's already tenuous supply lines. However, during his battalion's tour, 5 RAR conducted only one interdiction mission, Operation *Crows Nest*.

Logistics was the area that the Australians interdicted in Operation *New Life*, at FSB Coral and with the Minefield Barrier. However, these efforts were the exception; the need to undertake search and destroy and cordon and search missions prevented the task force from maintaining pressure on the enemy's logistics. Had the allies severed the junction between the village and the main force units, then both sides of the VC war effort, the cadres and the main force units, would either have had to confront the allies directly, or face extinction from lack of support.

Even had MACV and 1 ATF showed greater operational flexibility and a more adept willingness to challenge the existing intellectual structures, these changes would still not have been enough to make victory likely. What needed to be recognised was that insurgency wars operate primarily in the political not military sphere. Battlefield success means nothing if it is not accompanied by progress in winning the support of the local people. For the latter to occur the provision of good government is as important as that of security. When it intervened, the United States backed an undemocratic, corrupt, inefficient regime that lacked the support of the majority of the people. Even after Diem's assassination, the national government in Saigon remained at best irrelevant, at worst despised, in the lives of most of its citizens. The government needed massive remedial work if it was to win the loyalty of its people, but unfortunately, fixing the nation's governance never received the priority it needed, either from the United States or from Australia.

In 1971, VC main force units had a reduced presence in Phuoc Tuy. However, the communist cadre and village-level infrastructure, although weakened, remained active and was still capable of recruitment and regeneration. Despite six years of effort 1 ATF had not severed the insurgents' grip on the population, and the enemy's sanctuaries in the Long Hai, Nui May Tao and Nui Dinh hills remained intact. Nor had the Australians destroyed the enemy's village-level guerrilla platoons, and *D445 Provincial Mobile Battalion*, Phuoc Tuy's stalwart regional unit, continued to haunt the province. Once the Australians departed Nui Dat, the insurgents again moved into the open.

Vietnamisation

After Abrams succeeded Westmoreland as COMMACV he reassessed the direction of the American war effort. Tet and its ensuing shock waves resulted in the abandonment of the disgraced strategy of attrition and its replacement by Vietnamisation. The new strategy called for ARVN's upgrading through training and the provision of equipment. MACV's priority was now to prepare the ARVN to take over the fighting. The Americans continued to face the VC in battle, but now MACV's primary mission was not to defeat the enemy but to ready the ARVN for that task. In Phuoc Tuy the Australians also took on a greater training role. In May 1968 peace talks began in Paris, but immediately deadlocked with glacial progress.

In 1969 Richard Nixon succeeded Johnson as President of the United States. In part, his rise to power derived from the electorate's faith that he would find for the nation a way out of Vietnam. Nixon accepted that a precipitate withdrawal was not an option; it would have resulted in the immediate collapse of South Vietnam because of the unpreparedness of the ARVN. Instead, he chose a three-pronged path. American de-escalation relied on a combination of an increase in the ARVN's capability, the gradual withdrawal of troops, and a substitution of air power for ground strength.

The first contingent of 25,000 United States soldiers left Vietnam in mid-1969 and others followed. The withdrawal was not steady but marked by escalations of violence in a conflict that remained bloody and dangerous. In 1970 Nixon extended the war to Cambodia, attempting to destroy the sanctuaries and logistic network that the VC had created across the border from Vietnam. In 1972 the North tried to overrun the South in another nationwide offensive. There were few American ground troops left to help the ARVN, but the massive intervention of United States air power broke the communists' attack.

In 1973 the United States claimed what Nixon called 'peace with honour' at its talks with North Vietnam. While the Paris Peace Agreement provided the United States with a way out of the quagmire of South-East Asia, the policy of Vietnamisation proved a fiction. It had been impossible to make the ARVN into an effective military organisation, especially one capable of managing an opponent of the skill and determination of the North Vietnamese army. In addition, the political situation in Saigon remained chaotic and inefficient, and the local economy was on the brink of collapse, which further hindered military reforms. In 1975 the North stepped up the pressure on the South. Without the United States' ground and air support the GVN forces fell apart. On 30 April North Vietnamese troops entered Saigon and, as US helicopters spirited the lucky few from the roof of the American Embassy, the city fell to the communists.

Coming Home

Once the United States began to draw down its force numbers in Vietnam, the Australian government also decided to begin its own withdrawal. This was to be a gradual process of progressive troop reductions as, following the objectives of Vietnamisation of the war effort, 1 ATF handed over greater responsibility for security in Phuoc Tuy to the South Vietnamese. The MATT team initiative was part of this process.

In April 1970, Prime Minister Gorton announced that the government would not replace 8 RAR when it returned home at the end of its tour, thereby reducing 1 ATF to a two-battalion formation. The Centurion tanks were the next to leave, further reducing the task force's fighting strength. In August 1971 the government determined that the rest of the task force would return home by the end of the year. In October, 3 RAR departed, followed by 4 RAR/NZ, in November.

On 5 October 1971 the final COMATF, Brigadier Bruce McDonald left Nui Dat for the last time. Command of Australian ground forces in Phuoc Tau then passed to Colonel P. J. Greville, the commander of 1 ALSG. On 6 November 4 RAR handed Nui

Dat over to 946 Regional Force Company. A member of 4 RAR recalled as the South Vietnamese soldiers neared that 'they wore an assortment of uniform, civilian clothes, and webbing, all in varying degrees of shabbiness and disrepair.' The soldier continued, 'I think we felt overwhelmingly sorry for them. I think we all did.' The following day the Australian rearguard made its way to Vung Tau; the South Vietnamese in Phuoc Tuy were now on their own.

With the hand-over of Nui Dat, the main Australian presence in South Vietnam switched to Vung Tau. To help provide security for 1 ALSG, 4 RAR left behind D Company, however the infantry spent most of its time helping the logisticians to clean and pack the deployment's equipment and stores as the enemy made no effort to hinder the departure. In early 1972 the job was done and the soldiers of 1 ALSG sailed from Vung Tau for the long passage home.

The only Australian troops still remaining in Vietnam at this point were the advisers of the AATTV. The Team had been the first Australian unit to arrive in Vietnam and would be the last to leave. In mid-December 1972, on his election as Australia's new Prime Minister, Gough Whitlam ordered the remaining members of the Team back home. Australia's Vietnam War was at an end.

1 ATF's soldiers approach HMAS *Sydney* for the voyage home to Australia.
AWM FOD/72/0043/VN.

ABBREVIATIONS & ACRONYMS

AA	anti-aircraft		km	kilometre
AATTV	Australian Army Training Team Vietnam		LAD	Light Aid Detachment
			LMG	light machine-gun
adv	advance		LZ	landing zone
AFV	armoured fighting vehicle		m	metres
AK47	Avtomat Kalashnikova 47		MACV	Military Assistance Command, Vietnam
ALSG	Australian Logistic Support Group			
AO	area of operations		MATT	Mobile Advisory and Training Team
APC	armoured personnel carrier		MBT	main battle tank
ARVN	Army of the Republic of Vietnam		mg	machine-gun
ATF	Australian Task Force		mk	mark
AWM	Australian War Memorial		mm	millimetres
bhp	brake horse power		NATO	North Atlantic Treaty Organisation
bn	battalion			
CGS	Chief of the General Staff		NCO	non-commissioned officer
CIA	Central Intelligence Agency		NZ	New Zealand
CO	Commanding Officer		OR	other ranks
COMAAFV	Commander Australian Army Force Vietnam		PF	Popular Force
			PIR	Pacific Islands Regiment
COMAFV	Commander, Australian Force Vietnam		pl	platoon
			POW	prisoner of war
COMUSMACV	Commander, United States Military Assistance Command, Vietnam		PRC	People's Republic of China
			PWLH	Prince of Wales Light Horse
			RAAF	Royal Australian Air Force
CORDS	Civil Operations and Revolutionary Development Support		RAICM	Royal Australian Infantry Corps Museum
coy	company		RAN	Royal Australian Navy
det	detachment		RAR	Royal Australian Regiment
DMZ	Demilitarized Zone		recce	reconnaissance
DOW	died of wounds		RF	Regional Force
DRV	Democratic Republic of Vietnam (the North)		RNZA	Royal New Zealand Artillery
			RPD	Ruchnoy Pulemet Degtyarova
dwt	deadweight tonnage		RPG	rocket-propelled grenade
FAC	forward air controller		rpm	rounds per minute
FFV	Field Force Vietnam		RVN	Republic of Vietnam
FO	forward observer		SAS	Special Air Service
FSB	fire support base		SEATO	South-East Asia Treaty Organisation
g	grams			
GPMG	general purpose machine-gun		sec	second
GS	general service		shp	shaft horse power
GVN	Government of Vietnam (the South)		SLR	self-loading rifle
GVW	gross vehicle weight		TAOR	tactical area of responsibility
HE	high explosive		US	United States
HEAT	high explosive anti-tank		USMC	United States Marine Corps
HQ	headquarters		USSR	Union of Soviet Socialist Republics
Indep	independent		VC	Viet Cong
kg	kilogram		VC	Victoria Cross
KIA	killed in action		WIA	wounded in action
kph	kilometre per hour		WO	warrant officer

BIBLIOGRAPHY

Unpublished Sources:

The Australian War Memorial (AWM) has a large collection of Vietnam War official and private records. Collections examined include: AWM 95; AWM 98; AWM 102; AWM 103; AWM 107; AWM 117; AWM 279; O'Brien Collection, PR88/91; and Serong Collection, PR00639.

The Royal Australian Infantry Corps Museum provided access to their collection of Vietnam era weapons.

Published Sources:

Anderson, David L., *The Vietnam War*, Palgrave, Basingstoke, UK, 2005.
Anderson, Paul, *When the Scorpion Stings: The History of the 3rd Cavalry Regiment, Vietnam, 1965-1972*, Allen & Unwin, Crows Nest, 2002.
Australian Army, *Aid to the Civil Power*, Canberra, 1964.
_____, *The Enemy*, Canberra, 1964.
_____, *The Division in Battle, Pamphlet No. 11, Counter Revolutionary Warfare*, Army Headquarters, Canberra, 1965.
_____, *Pocket Books: South Vietnam*, Canberra, 1967.
_____, *Training Information Bulletin, No. 17, Airmobile Operations*, Department of Military Training.
_____, *The Enemy*, Army Headquarters, Canberra, 1970.
_____, *The Enemy, Amendment List No. 3, Bunker Systems*, Army Headquarters, Canberra, 1970.
_____, *Field Engineering, Pamphlet No. 7, Booby Traps: Parts 1 and 2*, Army Headquarters, Canberra, 1972.
_____, *Manual of Land Warfare, Part 1, Volume 3, Pamphlet No. 1, Counter-Insurgency Operations*, Department of Defence, Army Office, Canberra, 1980.
Australian Military Forces, *Ambush and Counter Ambush*, 1965.
_____, *Patrolling and Tracking*, 1965.
Barclay, Glen St J., *A Very Small Insurance Policy: Politics of Australian Involvement in Vietnam, 1954-1967*, University of Queensland Press, St Lucia, 1988.
Battle, M. R. (ed.), *The Year of the Tigers: The Second Tour of 5th Battalion, The Royal Australian Regiment in South Vietnam, 1969-70*, Printcraft Press, Brookvale, NSW, 1987.
Blair, Anne, *Ted Serong: The Life of an Australian Counter-Insurgency Expert*, Oxford University Press, Melbourne, 2002.
Bourke, J. R., 'Platoon Organisation, Rations and Equipment', *Australian Army Journal*, no. 208, September 1966, pp. 3-9.
Breen, Bob, *First to Fight: Australian Diggers, N.Z. Kiwis and U.S. Paratroopers in Vietnam, 1965-66*, The Battery Press, Nashville, 1988.
Buick, Bob, *All Guts and No Glory: The Story of a Long Tan Warrior*, Allen & Unwin, St Leonards, 2000.
Bushby, R. N., *Educating an Army: Australian Army Doctrinal Development and the Operational Experience in South Vietnam, 1965-1972*, SDSC, Canberra, 1998.
Chambers, John Whiteclay II, *The Oxford Companion to American Military History*, Oxford University Press, New York, 1999.
Chandler, R. M., 'Platoon Ambush', *Infantry*, May 1970, pp. 16-17.
Church, J.M., *Second to None: 2 RAR as the ANZAC Battalion in Vietnam, 1970-71*, Army Doctrine Centre, Mosman, 1996.
Clark, J. A., 'A Year in AATTV 1970', *Infantry*, January– February 1973, pp. 32-36.
Coates, H. J., 'The Armoured Personnel Carrier in Vietnam', *Infantry*, May–June 1972.
Collins, James Lawton, Jr., *The Development and Training of the South Vietnamese Army, 1950-1972*, Department of Army, Washington DC, 1975.

Commonwealth Parliamentary Debates (House of Representatives) (1964), pp. 2715-2718.

Daley, D., 'The Bunker World of the Viet Cong', *Infantry*, January 1971, pp. 26-31.

Dennis, Peter, et.al., *The Oxford Companion to Australian Military History*, Oxford University Press, Melbourne, 1997.

D'Hage, A. S., 'Company Attack on a Bunker System', *Infantry*, May 1970, pp. 28-29.

Duiker, William J., *Historical Dictionary of Vietnam*, The Scarecrow Press, Metuchen, NJ, 1989.

Essex-Clark, John, *Maverick Soldier: An Infantryman's Story*, Melbourne University Press, Melbourne, 1991.

Fall, Bernard B., *Hell in a Very Small Place: The Siege of Dien Bien Phu*, Da Capo Press, New York, 1967.

_____, *Street Without Joy*, Stackpole Books, Mechanicsburg, PA, 1994.

Freemantle, A. W., 'Patrol Lessons in Vietnam', *Army Journal*, no. 297, February 1974, pp. 43-59.

Frost, Frank, *Australia's War in Vietnam*, Allen & Unwin, Sydney, 1987.

Gardiner, T., 'Mobile Army Training Team', *Infantry*, September, 1970.

Giap, Vo Nguyen, *Banner of People's War: The Party's Military Line*, Pall Mall Press, London, 1970.

Grandin, Bob, *The Battle of Long Tan*, Allen & Unwin, Crows Nest, 2004.

Gration, Peter, 'On 1 ATF in Vietnam', *Journal of the Australian War Memorial*, no. 12, April 1988, pp. 45-46.

Greville, P. J., *The Royal Australian Engineers 1945 to 1972: Paving the Way*, Corps Committee of the Royal Australian Engineers, Moorebank, NSW, 2002.

Grey, Jeffrey, *A Military History of Australia*, Cambridge University Press, Melbourne, 1999.

Hall, Robert A., *Combat Battalion: The Eighth Battalion in Vietnam*, Allen & Unwin, St Leonards, 2000.

Ham, Paul, *Vietnam: The Australian War*, HarperCollins Publishers, Sydney, 2007.

Hammett, A. W., 'More About Bunkers', *Infantry*, September 1970, pp. 8-13.

Hartley, J. C., 'The Platoon Commander's War', in John Mordike (ed.), *The RAAF in the War in Vietnam: The Proceedings of the 1998 RAAF History Conference*, Air Power Studies Centre, Fairbairn, ACT, 1999, pp. 19-31.

_____, 'The Australian Army Training Team Vietnam', in Peter Dennis and Jeffrey Grey, *The Australian Army and the Vietnam War, 1962-1972, The 2002 Chief of Army's Military History Conference*, Army History Unit, Canberra, 2002, pp. 240-47.

Horner, D. M., *Australian Higher Command in the Vietnam War*, SDSC, Canberra, 1986.

_____, *Duty First: The Royal Australian Regiment in War and Peace*, Allen & Unwin, North Sydney, 1990.

_____, *SAS Phantoms of the Jungle: A History of the Australian Special Air Service*, Allen & Unwin, Crows Nest, 2002.

_____, *Strategic Command: General Sir John Wilton and Australia's Asian Wars*, Oxford University Press, Melbourne, 2005.

Jensen, A. H., 'FSB Coral', *Infantry*, May–June 1973, pp. 25-31.

Khan, C. N., 'A Tough Nut to Crack', *Infantry*, January 1970.

Kolko, Gabriel, *Anatomy of a War: Vietnam, the United States, and the Modern Historical Experience*, Pantheon Books, New York, 1985.

Krepinevich, Andrew F. Jr., *The Army and Vietnam*, The Johns Hopkins University Press, Baltimore, 1989.

Kuring, Ian, 'Australian Task Force Operations in South Vietnam, 1966-1971', in Peter Dennis and Jeffrey Grey, *The Australian Army and the Vietnam War, 1962-1972, The 2002 Chief of Army's Military History Conference*, Army History Unit, Canberra, 2002, pp. 126-37.

_____, *Redcoats to Cams: A History of Australian Infantry, 1788-2001*, Australian Military History Publications, Loftus, 2004.

Larson, Stanley Robert and James Lawton Collin Jr., *Allied Participation in Vietnam*, Department of Army, Washington, 1975.

Lennon, W. W., 'Engineer Support in Vietnam', *Australian Army Journal*, no. 236, January 1969, pp. 3-18.

Mao, Tse-Tung, *Basic Tactics*, Pall Mall Press, London, 1967.

McAulay, Lex, *The Battle of Long Tan*, Arrow Books, Milsons Point, 1987.

_____, *The Battle of Coral*, Arrow Books, Milsons Point, 1988.

McDonagh, J. F., 'Civil Affairs in Phuoc Tuy Province, South Vietnam 1967-68', *Australian Army Journal*, no. 231, August 1968, pp. 3-15.

McKay, Gary, *In Good Company: One Man's War in Vietnam*, Allen & Unwin, North Sydney, 1991.

_____, *Jungle Tracks: Australian Armour in Vietnam*, Allen & Unwin, St Leonards, 2001.

McNeill, Ian, 'An Outline of Australian Military Involvement in Vietnam: July 1962 – December 1972', *Defence Force Journal*, September 1980, pp. 42-53.

_____, *The Team: Australian Army Advisers in Vietnam, 1962-1972*, Australian War Memorial, Canberra, 1984.

_____, 'The Australian Army and the Vietnam War', in Peter Pierce, Jeffrey Grey and Jeff Doyle (eds.), *Vietnam Days: Australia and the Impact of Vietnam*, Penguin, Ringwood, Vic, 1991, pp. 11-61.

_____, *To Long Tan: The Australian Army and the Vietnam War, 1950-1966*, Australian War Memorial, Canberra, 1993.

_____ and Ashley Ekins, *On the Offensive: The Australian Army in the Vietnam War, January 1967–June 1968*, Allen & Unwin in Association with the Australian War Memorial, Crows Nest, 2003.

Nagl, John A., *Learning to Eat Soup with a Knife: Counterinsurgency Lessons from Malaya and Vietnam*, The University of Chicago Press, Chicago, 2005.

Newman, K. E., *The Anzac Battalion*, Printcraft Press, Brookvale, NSW, 1968.

O'Brien, Michael, *Conscripts and Regulars: With the Seventh Battalion in Vietnam*, Allen & Unwin, St Leonards, 1995.

O'Neill Robert, 'Three Villages of Phuoc Tuy', *Quadrant*, vol. XI, no. 1, January-February 1967, pp. 4-10.

_____, *Vietnam Task: The 5ᵗʰ Battalion, Royal Australian Regiment*, Cassell, Melbourne, 1968.

_____, 'Australian Military Problems in Vietnam', *Australian Outlook*, vol. 23, no. 1, April 1969, pp. 46-57.

Palmer, Dave R., *Summons of the Trumpet: U.S. – Vietnam in Perspective*, Presidio Press, Novato, CA, 1978.

Perriman, A., 'The Battle of Binh Ba, June 1969', *Infantry*, September 1969, pp. 5-7.

Pike, Douglas, *Viet Cong: The Organization and Techniques of the National Liberation Front of South Vietnam*, MIT Press, Cambridge, 1967.

Rothwell, Peter, 'The Attack at Duc Hanh', *Infantry*, September 1971, pp. 14-17.

'Search and Clear Operations', *Australian Army Journal*, no. 208, September 1966, pp. 42-44.

Smith, Barry, 'The Role and Impact of Civil Affairs in South Vietnam 1965-1971', in Peter Dennis and Jeffrey Grey, *The Australian Army and the Vietnam War, 1962-1972, The 2002 Chief of Army's Military History Conference*, Army History Unit, Canberra, 2002, pp. 229-39.

Stanton, Shelby, L., *The Rise and Fall of an American Army: U.S. Ground Forces in Vietnam, 1965-1973*, Spa Books, Stevenage, Herts, 1989.

Stapleton, Thomas, 'A New Role for the Australian Army?', *Australian Outlook*, vol. 25, no. 3, December 1971, pp. 3-12.

Stretton, Alan, *Soldier in a Storm: An Autobiography*, Collins, Sydney, 1978.

Summers, Harry G., *Vietnam War Almanac*, Facts on File, New York, 1985.

Welburn, M. C. J., *The Development of Australian Army Doctrine: 1945-1964*, SDSC, Canberra, 1994.

Wiest, Andrew, *The Vietnam War, 1956-1975*, Osprey Publishing, Oxford, 2002.

Wilensky, Robert J., *Military Medicine to Win Hearts and Minds*, Texas Tech University Press, Lubbock, TX, 2004.

Williams, Clive, 'Doctrine, Training and Combat with 1ˢᵗ Battalion, The Royal Australian Regiment, 1965-1966', in Peter Dennis and Jeffrey Grey, *The Australian Army and the Vietnam War, 1962-1972, The 2002 Chief of Army's Military History Conference*, Army History Unit, Canberra, 2002, pp. 116-25.

Williams, Iain McLean, *Vietnam: A Pictorial History of the Sixth Battalion The Royal Australian Regiment*, Printcraft Press, Brookvale, NSW, 1967.

FURTHER READING

Australian Focus

Ian McNeill, *To Long Tan: The Australian Army and the Vietnam War 1950-1966*, Allen & Unwin, St Leonards, 1993; and Ian McNeill and Ashley Ekins, *On the Offensive: The Australian Army and the Vietnam War 1967-1968*, Allen & Unwin, Crows Nest, 2003.

These works are part of the official history series of South-East Asian conflicts and cover the first half of Australia's land operations in Vietnam. While requiring a degree of commitment to finish, they often offer perceptive insights into the war, and are currently the final word on Australia's role in the conflict. Other volumes in the series cover the air, sea, medical and political aspects of the war. A third volume completing the story of the ground war is under preparation.

Peter Dennis and Jeff Grey (eds.), *The Australian Army and the Vietnam War*, Army History Unit, Canberra, 2002.

This work documents the proceedings of the 2002 Chief of Army's Military History Conference. The authors include overseas experts, academics and former officers. Among the offerings are: Roger Spiller, 'The Vietnam Syndrome: A Brief History'; John Coates, 'Preparing Armoured Units for Overseas Service'; and Michael O'Brien, 'The Training of the Australian Army Units for Active Service in Vietnam: the 7th Battalion, The Royal Australian Regiment'. This is a fine collection of essays and is worthy of consideration.

David Horner, *Australian Higher Command in the Vietnam War*, SDSC, Canberra, 1986.

Horner's focus is the high end of the art of war. He contrasts the expertise of 1 ATF in waging the war in Phuoc Tuy with the lack of direction and control emanating from Canberra. This work is essential reading for an understanding of Australia's strategic objectives in Vietnam and the higher problems of conflict management.

Frank Frost, *Australia's War in Vietnam*, Allen & Unwin, North Sydney, 1987.

Although Frost is not on sure ground when discussing operations and is unfamiliar with military terminology and procedure, the book retains value for its examination of the war at the policy level.

Richard Bushby, *Educating an Army: Australian Army Doctrinal Development and the Operational Experience in South Vietnam, 1965-1972*, SDSC, Canberra, 1998.

The evolution of the art of war and the processes by which military organisations recognise, decide upon and implement change are key issues for all professional military commanders. The focus of Bushby's slim volume is the evolution of Australian tactics and doctrine in Vietnam. He covers topics and issues that will be of interest to all contemporary military leaders.

Glen St J. Barclay, *A Very Small Insurance Policy: The Politics of Australian Involvement in Vietnam, 1954-1967*, University of Queensland Press, St Lucia, 1988.

This work examines Australia's national security policy and the government's efforts to interest the United States in the South-East Asian region. As the book's title suggests, the price of securing American support was involvement in Vietnam. From this perspective alone this work should be of interest to contemporary policy-makers and strategists.

Paul Ham, *Vietnam: The Australian War*, Harper Collins, Pymble, 2007.

Ham's good narrative style makes this an easy book to read but it is marred by inattention to detail and an overly ambitious objective. The definitive work on Australia and the Vietnam War has yet to be written.

'Two APCs, LAD, Nui Dat', Bruce Fletcher. Fibre-tipped pen.
AWM ART40449.

General Studies

Bernard B. Fall, *Street Without Joy*, Stackpole Books, Mechanicsburg, PA, 1994.

First published in 1961, *Street Without Joy* is one of the masterpieces of Vietnam War historiography. While focused on the French conflict, its lessons resonate with the American period. If American commanders had read this book the war may have ended differently. *Street Without Joy* is an essential read for all serious students of the Vietnam War or any other counter-insurgency conflict. Fall's companion book, *Hell in a Very Small Place: The Siege of Dien Bien* Phu (Harper & Row Publishers, New York, 1967) is also recommended.

David L. Anderson, *The Vietnam War*, Palgrave Macmillan, Basingstoke, Hampshire, 2005.

This book provides a short but excellent introduction to the Vietnam War. Anderson's interest lies in the conflict's political dimensions, and it covers all the key turning points from the French period to the American defeat. The book can stand on its own or provide the foundation for further study.

Andrew F. Krepinevich, Jr., *The Army and Vietnam*, The Johns Hopkins University Press, Baltimore, 1986.

Krepinevich, a United States Army officer, has produced a detailed, compelling and troubling account of what went wrong with the United States Army in Vietnam. At its core *The Army and Vietnam* is about the role of institutional culture in a military organisation's ability to meet and react to the challenges of war. America lost, Krepinevich argues, because its army went to war without an appropriate ethos for the waging of counter-insurgency warfare, and its commanders lacked the willingness and strength of character to make the necessary changes in their force's institutional culture.

191

John A. Nagl, *Learning to Eat Soup with a Knife: Counterinsurgency Lessons from Malaya and Vietnam*, University of Chicago Press, Chicago, 2005.

The author, an American officer and veteran of the war in Iraq, examines the Malayan Emergency and the Vietnam War to discover how military organisations learn to fight conflicts for which they are not initially prepared. This is mandatory counter-insurgency reading.

Shelby L. Stanton, *The Rise and Fall of an American Army: U.S. Ground Forces in Vietnam, 1965-1973*, Spa Books, Stevenage, Herts, 1989.

When American combat troops arrived in Vietnam in 1965 they represented the vanguard of a well-organised, -led, and -equipped fighting machine. At the conflict's end the Army had been reduced to a shell that was unfit for combat and required extensive reorganisation as a volunteer force. Stanton's book charts this transformation.

Douglas Pike, *PAVN: People's Army of Vietnam*, Presidio Press, Novato, CA, 1986.

Pike, an accomplished scholar of insurgency warfare and the North Vietnamese armed forces, outlines the origins, organisation, ideology and strategy of what he terms 'the Prussians of Asia'. This book is essential reading for an understanding of the strengths and weaknesses of the 'other side of the hill'.

James H. Willbanks, *The Tet Offensive: A Concise History*, Columbia University Press, New York, 2007.

A good introduction to the subject of Tet which places the campaign in its political and military context. Willbanks also offers a useful analysis of the media's responsibility in shaping the outcome of the battle.

Australian Unit Studies

Ian McNeill, *The Team: Australian Army Advisors in Vietnam, 1962-1972*, Australian War Memorial, Canberra, 1984.

This book provides the definitive account of Australia's advisory efforts in Vietnam by the conflict's official historian.

Robert J. O'Neill, *Vietnam Task: The 5th Battalion, Royal Australian Regiment*, Cassell, Melbourne, 1968.

O'Neill served as a company commander with 5 RAR in Vietnam and after the end of his military career went on to become a widely respected academic scholar. His talents in both professions are evident in this work. O'Neill has produced the finest unit history of Australian service in Vietnam to date. If you can read only one unit history it should be this one.

Bob Breen, *First to Fight: Australian Diggers, N.Z. Kiwis and U.S. Paratroopers in Vietnam, 1965-66*, The Battery Press, Nashville, 1988.

This is one of the better Australian unit histories. Breen tells the story of 1 RAR's association with 173 Airborne Brigade (Separate) in Bien Hoa Province.

Robert Hall, *Combat Battalion: The Eighth Battalion in Vietnam*, Allen & Unwin, St Leonards, 2000.

While the focus of Hall's analysis is 8 RAR, this work goes far beyond that of a simple retelling of the battalion's operations. Instead, Hall deals with the full range of the Vietnam experience, discussing topics such as maintenance of morale, personal response to combat, and unit cohesion.

Memoirs and Recollections

J. C. Hartley, 'The Platoon Commander's War' in John Mordike (ed.), *The RAAF in the War in Vietnam: The Proceedings of the 1998 RAAF History Conference*, Air Power Studies Centre, Fairbairn, 1999, pp. 19-31.

This is a brief yet excellent insight into a rifle platoon commander's tour in Vietnam with 5 RAR, written by an officer who reached the army's highest ranks. This essay is well worth tracking down and reading.

Bob Buick, *All Guts and No Glory: The Story of a Long Tan Warrior*, Allen & Unwin, St Leonards, 2000.

Buick's book is a compelling page-turner that examines the author's year in Vietnam with 6 RAR. Buick covers the battalion's training and introduction to Vietnam, the Battle of Long Tan, and the aftermath of his wartime service.

Bob Grandin, *The Battle of Long Tan*, Allen & Unwin, Crows Nest, 2004.

Grandin served more as compiler of this book than author, and has brought together the memories of the officers who fought at Long Tan. Grandin was one of the RAAF helicopter pilots who resupplied D Company in the middle of the battle. This is an excellent company-eye view of the battle by those who fought and beat the VC.

Gary McKay, *In Good Company: One Man's War in Vietnam*, Allen & Unwin, North Sydney, 1987.

McKay entered the army as a national serviceman, graduated from Scheyville as a second lieutenant, served a tour in Vietnam where he was seriously wounded, became a regular soldier and reached the rank of lieutenant-colonel. As a platoon commander McKay tells a richly detailed and observant story of Vietnam at the sharp end.

Illustrative Works

Osprey Publishing has produced a number of works on various aspects of the Vietnam War. Among the available titles are: Kevin Lyles, *Vietnam ANZACS: Australian & New Zealand Troops in Vietnam, 1962-72*; Philip Katcher, *Armies of the Vietnam War, 1962-75*; Mike Chappell, *Armies of the Vietnam War, vol. 2*; James R. Arnold, *The Tet Offensive, 1968*; Gordon L. Rottman, *US Army Infantryman in Vietnam, 1965-73*; Ed Gilbert, *The US Marine Corps in the Vietnam War*; Gordon L. Rottman, *Viet Cong and NVA Tunnels and Fortifications of the Vietnam War*; Gordon L. Rottman, *The US Army in the Vietnam War, 1965-73*; Gordon L. Rottman, *Vietnam Airmobile Warfare Tactics*; Gordon L. Rottman, *Khe Sanh, 1967-68*; and Andrew Wiest, *The Vietnam War, 1956-1975*.

INDEX